Inventioneering

Nurturing Intellectual Talent in the Classroom

by

Bob Stanish and Carol Singletary

illustrated by Janet Skiles

photography by Carol Singletary and Frank Crocker

GOOD APPLE, INC.
BOX 299
CARTHAGE, IL 62321-0299

Cover by Tom Sjoerdsma

ISBN No. 0-86653-402-4

Printing No. 987

GOOD APPLE, INC.
BOX 299
CARTHAGE, IL 62321-0299

ACKNOWLEDGEMENTS

Many thanks to Mark Singletary for some special technical assistance.

A special thanks to Frank Crocker for his photographs.

Also special thanks to a group of creative, inventive, problem-solving field testers from the Dickinson Independent School District, Dickinson, Texas:

Sammy Baisden
Jennifer Baker
Nancy Blasberg
Sean Buchanan
John Burrescia
Kimberly Cameron
Lisa Candelari
Darren Carney
Megan Casey
Robert Cernosek
Kevin Chappell
Robby Cole
Joseph Conwell
Michael Cormier
Erin Denney
Michael DeVall
Charlene Downey
John Doyle
Jill Farris
Marcus Fernandez
Jennifer Flex
Jason Franks
Ben Frazar
David Funk
Zoe Funk
Denise Garner
Michael Gasinski
Jeremy Gernand
Tara Gilbert
Amy Glidden
David Goldblum
David Griffith
Sean Hale
Kirk Harstad
Jennifer Hartenberger
Jessica Headrick
Robert Heflin
Aimee Heidt
Bart Hennigan
Brad Henry
Robert Hill
Walter Hokanson
Nannette Jackson
Brett Johnson
Vikki Johnson
B.J. Jones
Kris Jones
Michael Kulvicki
Jennifer Lairscey
Jon Luke
Katie Luke
Brook Mackey
Derek McBride
Sumor Medord
Kevin Mickens
Jason Minter
Angela Moehring
Quester Monday
Jennifer Naus
Nadia Nekooi
Allison Nelson
Mai Nguyen
Andrea Null
Rick Owens
Jason Pate
Eric Prescott
Jamie Price
Jennifer Pyle
Julie Richards
Andy Roeser
Jana Rose
Michelle Ross
Eric Rosser
Steve Schroeder
Katrina Seale
Stephen Shimek
Greg Sills
Brenden Steber
Chris Strom
Dana Stuart
Cindy Thomas
Natalie Thompson
Anita Tipps
Bonnie Trahan
Ryan Walter
Tommy Ware
Autumn White
Ellen Woods

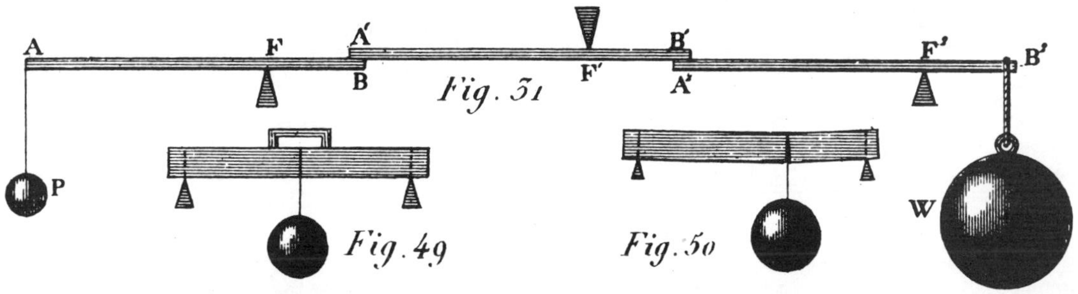

TABLE OF CONTENTS

Purpose . . . 1
Target Population . . . 2
Instructional Processes . . . 2
Step-by-Step Procedures . . . 7
For-the-Fun-of-It Procedures . . . 9
Sample Test Items . . . 13
Scientific Principles . . . 19
The Inventions
A Coat Hanger for All Reasons . . . 28
The Spaghetti-Eating Utensil . . . 30
Hilarious Huggables Who Hug Plants . . . 34
Shake Hands with U. NAMEIT . . . 38
The Pecan Contraption . . . 43
The Bedroom Picker-Upper . . . 46
Special Delivery . . . 50
Balloon Busters . . . 53
Invention Task Slips . . . 57
References and Suggested Readings . . . 60

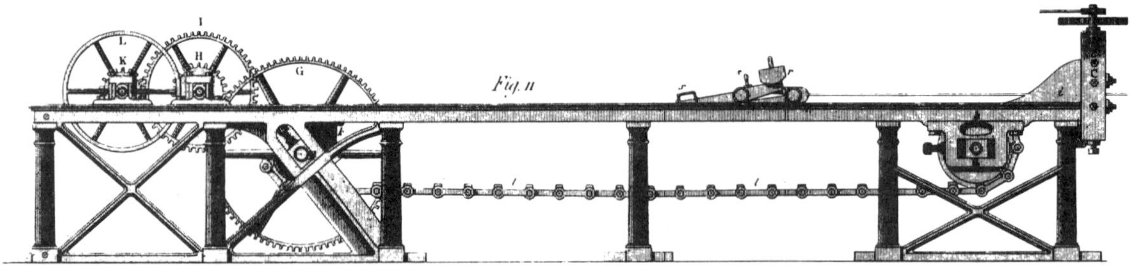

PURPOSE

Inventioneering may be applied as a unit of study within the broad scopes of the physical sciences. It may be applied, as well, as a means of supplementing an existing unit and a means of promoting the skills of creative thinking and problem solving.

THIS BOOK IS INTENDED TO . . .

expand the use of creative thinking and problem solving to provided problem situations.

encourage curiosity so that ideas are generated and expanded.

promote the completion of a product and to assess the approaches taken.

associate the products made with the underlying principles of science.

nurture a broad range of intellectual talent.

IN DOING SO, STUDENTS WILL BE . . .

engaged in diverging and converging thought processes.

engaged in extending their ideation through modification and other techniques of questioning.

engaged in searching for unique solutions to a given problem.

engaged in refining products.

engaged in challenging concepts through the higher thought processes.

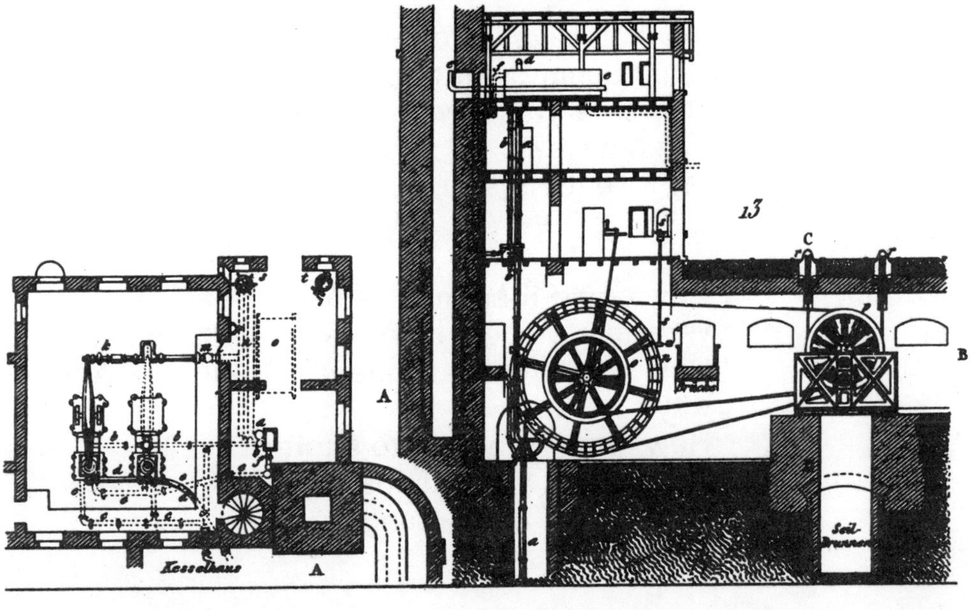

TARGET POPULATION

Inventioneering will accommodate, with appropriate modification, grades 3 through 9.

The most appropriate usage would be for children who . . .

are placed in gifted and talented classrooms.

are gifted, creative or talented in general classrooms.

are involved in creative problem solving (Osborn-Parnes Method).

are involved in or have been involved in *Odyssey of the Mind*, formerly *Olympics of the Mind; Future Problem Solving Bowls* or similar competitive events stimulating creative thinking and problem solving.

are suspected of having unique and unusual intellectual talents but are placed in classrooms where science equipment is limited.

INSTRUCTIONAL PROCESSES

It is important that teachers employ QUESTIONING TECHNIQUES that rely on:

Open-Endedness:
"What else might work?"
"Other functions?"
"In what ways could it be improved?"
"What other choices did you consider?"

Analogies:
"In what ways is your invention like a thunderstorm?"
"What common attributes does it have with a chair?"
"Compare your invention with a flashlight battery. How much alike?"
"My invention is to a _______ as a _______ is to a _______."

Modification:
"How could it be made smaller? Larger?"
"What parts could be replaced with something else?"
"How might it be reversed? Modified? Altered in some way?"
"How might it be put to another use?"
"What could you eliminate?"
"What could be rearranged?"

BRAINSTORMING

Whenever possible, introduce an activity problem by having students brainstorm either in a large group, small group or individually as many ideas as possible. As an example from the activity "A Coat Hanger for All Reasons" are these student responses:

PROBLEM: How many different uses for a coat hanger?

light bulb remover
airport wind sock
turn on/off TV from distance
open a locked car door
attach magnet for metal pickup
axle for small-wheeled carriers
binocular holders
pajama strap finder
drawer dividers
handle for big dollhouse
book holder
small basketball hoop
jewelry item holder
weather vane
holder for loop earrings
frame for linen lunch box
bath towel holder
badminton frame
slingshot
frame for rag doll
bicycle basket
clock hands
hot plate stand
wire sculpture
dipstick for Easter eggs
Christmas tree stand
bicycle stand
hanging pot hooks
doorstop
conductor's baton
musical instrument
bird feeder stand
plant stand
string instrument piece
umbrella frame
oil dipstick
holder for yard signs
gate hinges
cookie cutter
fireplace poker
paint stirrer
gate latch
sundial
dog leash
shoe rack
muzzle for a dog
a bow
parts for a mobile
use for hanging ornaments
kite frame
rain gauge
butterfly net frame
depth stick measure
paint roller holder
portable fishing pole
permanent chopsticks
shish kebab skewer
stakes for tent
a hat rack
giant safety pin
large paper clip
shoe scraper
dish holder
cartridge holder
tool holder
lunch box organizer
back scratcher
hot dog stick
planting pot rake
make home address numbers
wire cage handle
lightning rod
for feeding angry alligators
marshmallow stick
newspaper rack
gun barrel cleaner
sheet music holder
spare button holder
soap bubble maker
storing washers
walkman holder
twists for garbage bags
nail puller

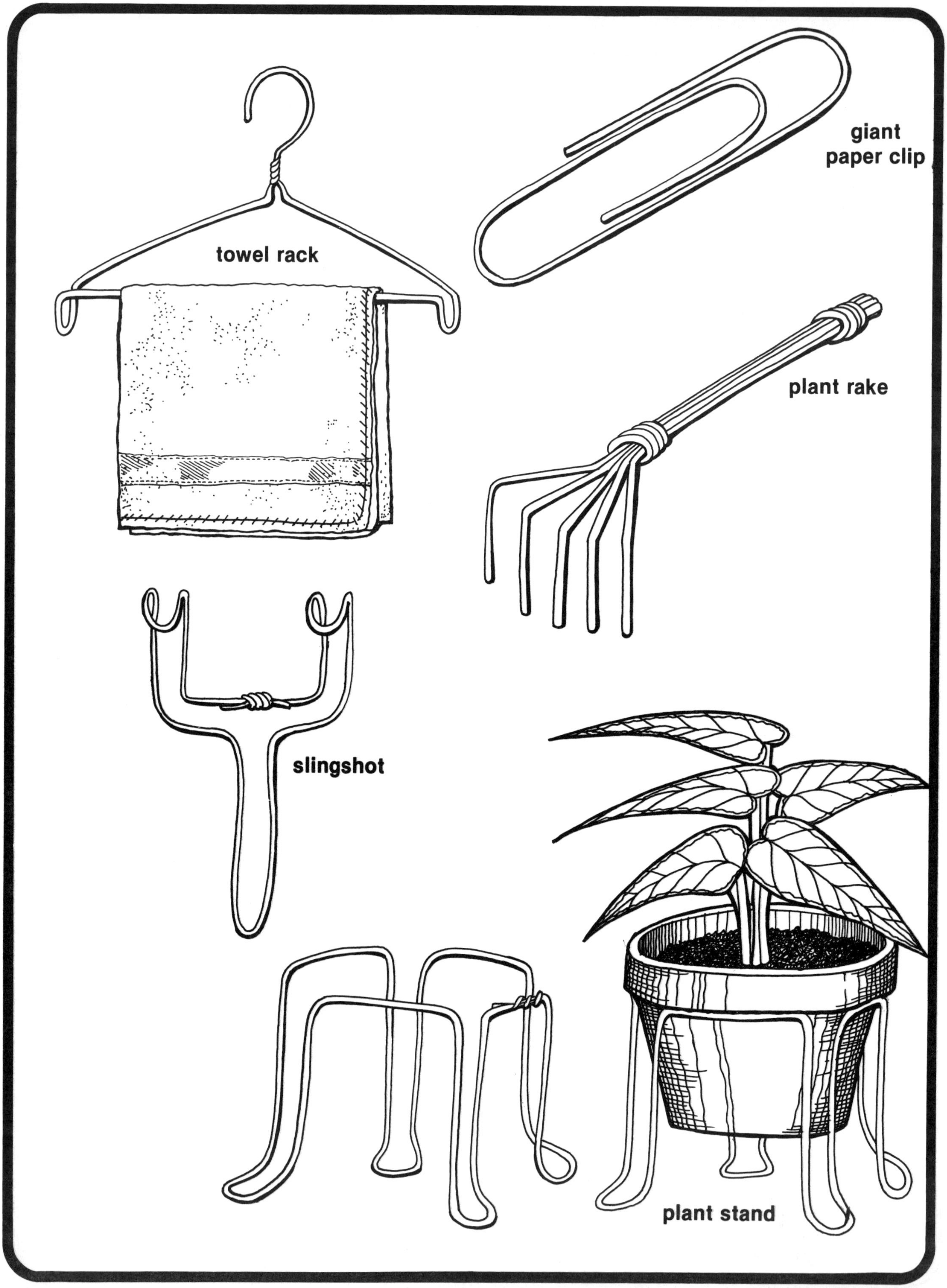
towel rack
giant
paper clip
plant rake
slingshot
plant stand

It can be noted from the brainstormed list of ideas that some ideas would have the potential for ridicule in many classrooms. Ridicule can be intimidating to the extent of slowing the flow of ideas. Ridicule was not experienced in the pilot study. Time was spent with students on the value and acceptance of all ideas—both unusual and unique.

Brainstorming and the techniques of brainstorming are diverging kinds of processes. To sort out the most promising ideas requires a converging process.

CRITERION

The ideas on the preceding page are massive. What is needed is a way to discriminate and converge on the most workable and potentially rewarding ideas. It is suggested, as an idea-sorting device, that students simply apply numerical ratings of importance to the ideas brainstormed. A scale such as this would work effectively: 3 points = good; 2 points = fair; 1 point = poor. The emphasis here is to converge the many ideas into a more workable listing of fewer ideas.

The next step is to select **criteria** by which the ideas favored may be applied. It is suggested for the purposes of this book that criteria should include anywhere between four and five items. Some criteria which might be considered would include the following:

- ease of doing
- cost
- safety
- works consistently
- quality of design
- durable
- attractive
- school policies
- construction time
- set-up time
- suits the problem
- available parts and materials
- enjoyable
- useful

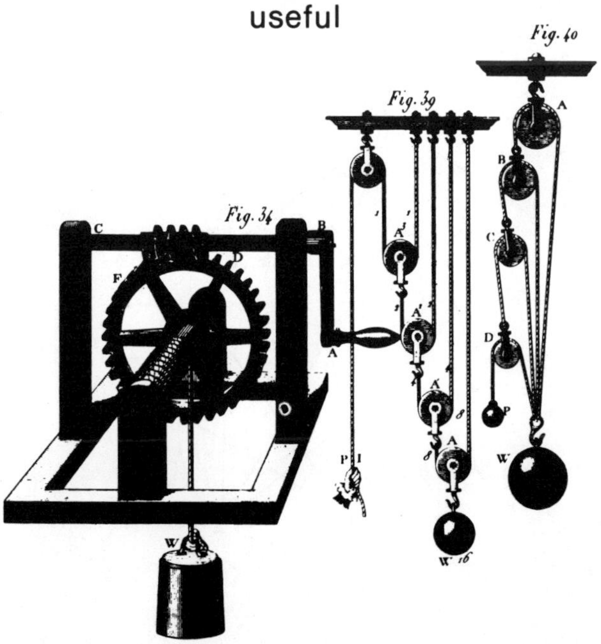

The four or five selected criteria (see preceding page) should be written on a grid. These items are chosen on the basis of appropriateness to the problem or invention possibility.

The best ideas sorted are then written on the top spaces of the grid.

Starting with the first criterion item, judge each idea across the page. Award points to each idea. Use the point distribution recommended by the rating scale.

Proceed through the evaluation grid by moving to the second criterion. Award points accordingly with each criterion until the selected ideas have been evaluated. Total the number of points and enter that number under each column at the bottom of the grid. Ideas receiving the greatest number of points would be considered promising invention possibilities.

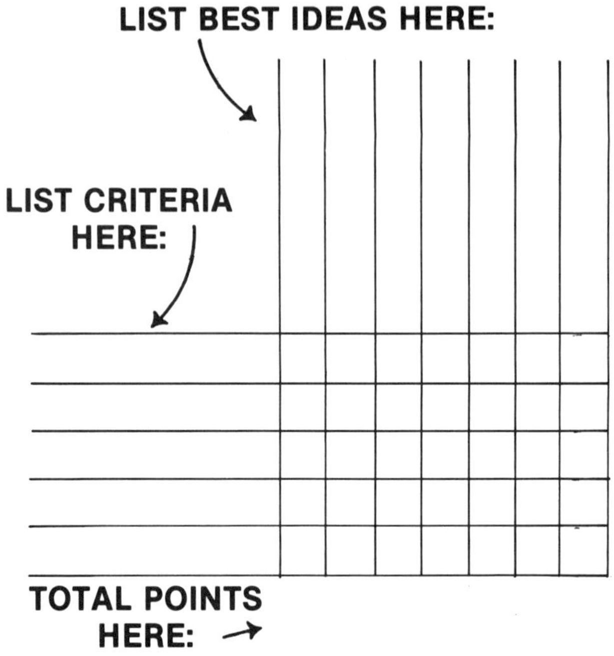

SUGGESTED RATE SCALE:

5 points = Excellent idea
4 points = Good idea
3 points = Average idea
2 points = Below average idea
1 point = Poor idea

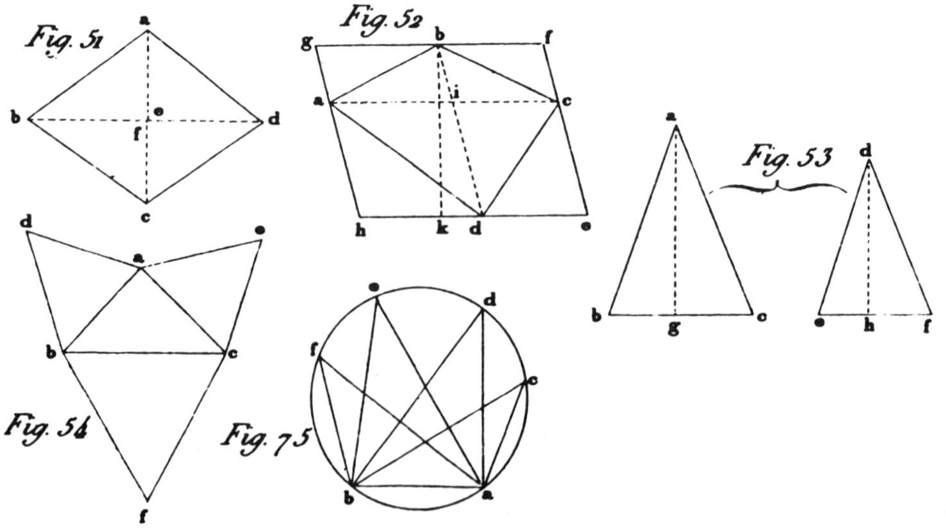

The major benefit of using a grid is to cause students to critically examine their ideas in association with established criteria. Some of the invention tasks in this book are more conductive to a grid than others. Encourage the use of the grid, whenever possible, with selected invention activities.

The photograph here depicts one student who selected two ideas to pursue the problem of how many different uses for a wire coat hanger? He selected the best ideas arbitrarily. These ideas were then placed on a grid. Criteria selected to evaluate the ideas included cost, consistent performance, quality of design, available parts and materials and attractiveness. The highest numerical ratings were registered on an airport wind sock and a small basketball hoop. The basketball hoop, incidently, can be placed above a waste can—a built-in motivator for picking up trash and paper from a floor.

Teacher assessment of invention products should be in relationship to the student-selected criteria. Don't impose a different criteria.

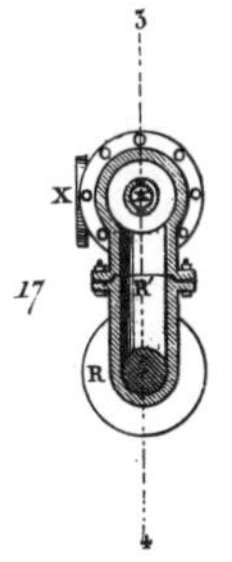

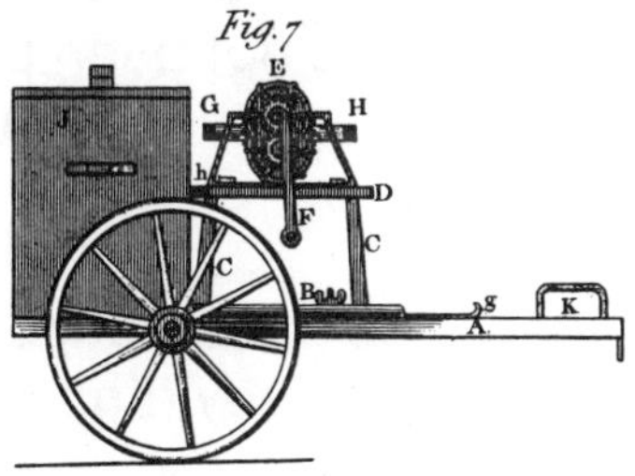

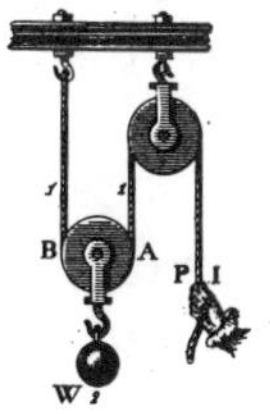

STEP-BY-STEP PROCEDURES

1. Select an invention task. There are **invention task slips** for each invention beginning on page 57. Duplicate the task selected and distribute copies to students. Determine the due date for the inventions. It is recommended that a two-week period of time be given for their completion. Inventions are to be completed at home.

OPTIONS FOR YOUNGER STUDENTS:

Teams: Allow students the option of teaming with another student on an invention.

Individual Effort: Students who want to create their own inventions should be encouraged to do so.

Individual and Team: Students who want to team with another student and still do a different approach for themselves should be allowed this option as well.

Caution: Encourage students to do the inventions themselves or with another student. Should dangerous tools be needed, have them enlist some adult assistance. Electrical and power tools should be handled by adults.

2. Review the activity page for the invention selected. Note the **general objective** and the related **sub-objectives.** These objectives are appropriate for placement in lesson plan books. Make sure that students fully understand the **conditions** under which the inventions are constructed and demonstrated.

3. Use classroom time to extend student thinking on invention possibilities. The **procedures** section of each activity format is for this purpose.

4. At the time of the invention demonstrations or shortly thereafter, have students determine the underlying scientific principles involved. There is a **Scientific Principles** section on page 19. Some inventions will undoubtedly feature some principles that have not been provided for in this section. It is suggested that teachers also consult available books in the physical sciences.

   It is suggested that students be encouraged to associate at least one principle involved with an invention. Providing investigative time in the school library will probably, in most cases, be adequate. Making available books and other reference materials in a classroom is still another way. A third alternative is to construct lessons based upon the principles provided in the **scientific principles** section.

5. Some classroom time should be devoted to some of the ideas presented in the activity section of **Multi-Disciplinary Expansions**. It is not suggested that all of these activities be employed. Select those that appeal to you as a teacher.

FOR-THE-FUN-OF-IT PROCEDURES

Inventioneering is a highly motivating unit in both creativity and the physical sciences. The objective of the authors, in addition to those cited in the purpose at the beginning of this book, was to allow children the experience, the joy, and the excitement of discovery through problem solving. What is provided here are some excursions that will accelerate the enjoyment of the learning.

Photographs: Enlist some parents or staff personnel or even yourself to take photographs—plenty of them! Staple them to bulletin boards in your room, in the library, or send copies home to parents. They become the best testimony for your efforts and the efforts of your students. They can become, also, a valuable learning reference for those students who will experience **inventioneering** in the years to come.

A Convention for Inventioneers: Take advantage of a wonderful opportunity for advancing school and parent involvement. Schedule a convention in which students demonstrate their inventions for parents. Begin the convention with "The Spaghetti-Eating Utensil" inventions. Ask a few parents to help organize a potluck spaghetti dinner at school. Begin the convention by having students demonstrate their inventions in the eating of spaghetti. Afterwards, provide time for the demonstrations of other student-made inventions.

STUDENT DRAWINGS AND OPERATORS' MANUALS

To nurture imagination, analysis, and synthesis, not to mention humor, have students illustrate or design or write descriptive images of some invention topics.

The Pecan Contraption

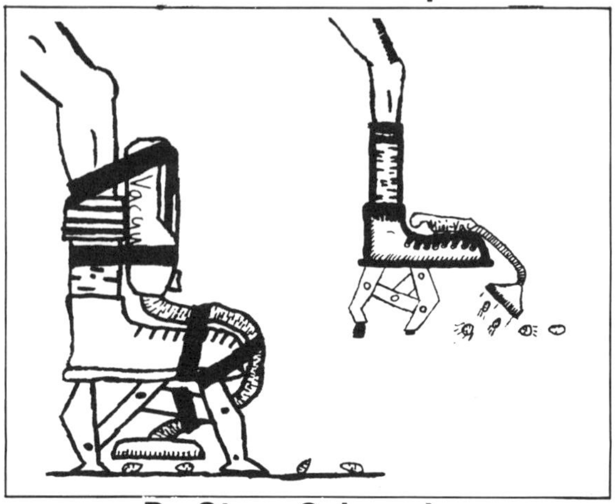

By Steve Schroeder

A FEW SUGGESTED TOPICS:

1. Any invention problem in this book
2. A homework machine
3. An antigravity machine
4. A bad taste detector
5. A pet finder
6. A fail-safe skateboard
7. Boring-day-at-school alarm
8. A nonspill school cafeteria tray
9. An all-weather hat for serious joggers
10. A Halloween hat with three different faces in one, but only one face is seen at a given time, in other words, a way to trick-or-treat at the same house three different times with the same mask
11. A device for detecting the location of lost items
12. A device for getting tennis balls down from the roofs of school buildings
13. A portable device for eating ice-cream cones that would not allow the ice cream to melt and drip on fingers, arms or clothes
14. A teacher robot that performs all classroom functions
15. A device for washing your face, combing your hair, and brushing your teeth at the same time
16. A gentle wake-up machine that functions without sound
17. A safety control hat for pedestrian traffic
18. A grocery cart with multifunctions

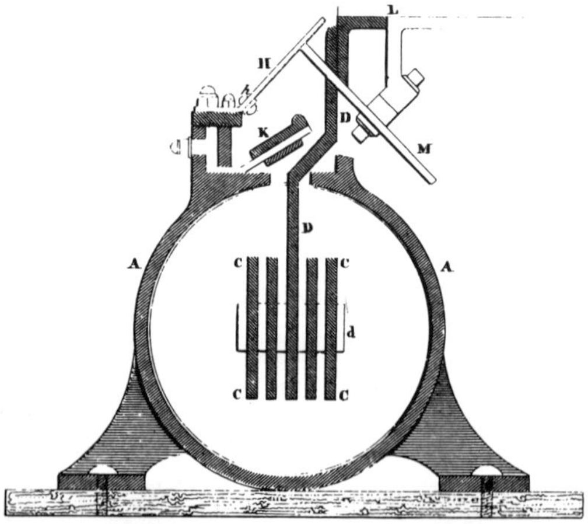

THE LUNCHEON CIRCUIT: Make arrangements with local civic and business organizations to take some of your young inventors to lunch in return for a slot on their programs. Most groups are looking for program speakers.

AFTER THE INVENTION DEMONSTRATION, THEN WHAT?

Occasionally offer one of these suggestions to your students:

1. Set up your invention in another area of the school. Place a tape recorder by it explaining the step-by-step procedures of how it works. Invite others to try it; then observe without comment.

2. Draw a cartoon sequence that explains the invention step by step.

3. Present your invention in pantomime. You be the invention!

4. Draw a flow chart of your invention on poster board.

5. Write and perform a play. Include your invention as one of the main props or characters.

6. Prepare a time line of events on paper that took your invention from an idea to a product.

7. Create an ad for your invention.

8. Write song lyrics about your invention to an already established tune.

9. Interview a patent attorney for the steps necessary in gaining a patent.

10. Check with a local business store and see if your invention along with a written description of it might be placed on display in a lobby or store window.

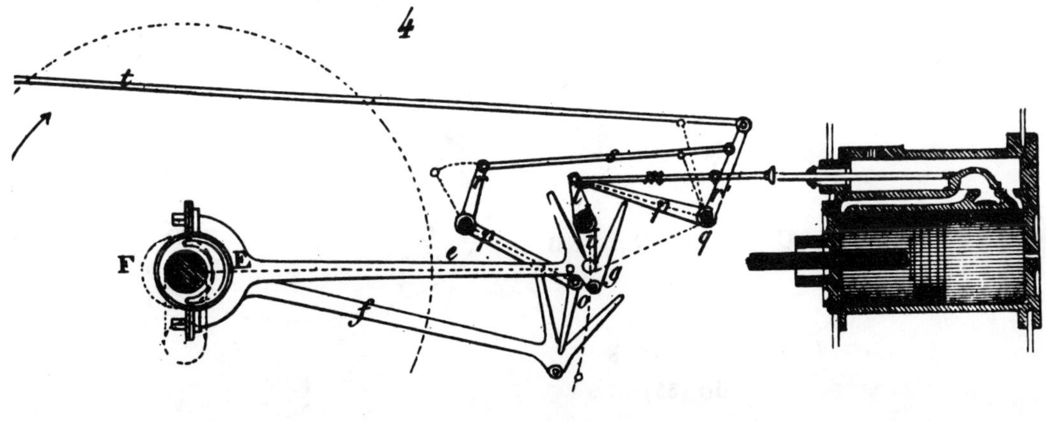

LEARNING CENTERS CREATED BY STUDENTS FOR STUDENTS

Assign small groups of students the responsibility of creating and displaying weekly learning centers. Each learning center featured for a week would display information, drawings, and posters about a famous inventor and an invention.

Some possible starters might include:

1. Vladimir Zworykin and the iconoscope.
2. Peter Mark Roget and either the Thesaurus or slide rule or calculating machine.
3. Jacques-Yves Cousteau and either the aqua-lung or the underseas lab.
4. Jan E. Matzeliger and the shoe assembly machine.
5. George Eastman and coated dry plates used in cameras.
6. Robert Watson-Watt and radar.

After a period of time, challenge students to determine their own inventor subject for a learning center.

ASSESSMENT

Assessment of student learnings from this book should reflect both process and content. Some suggestions on test items are provided on page 13.

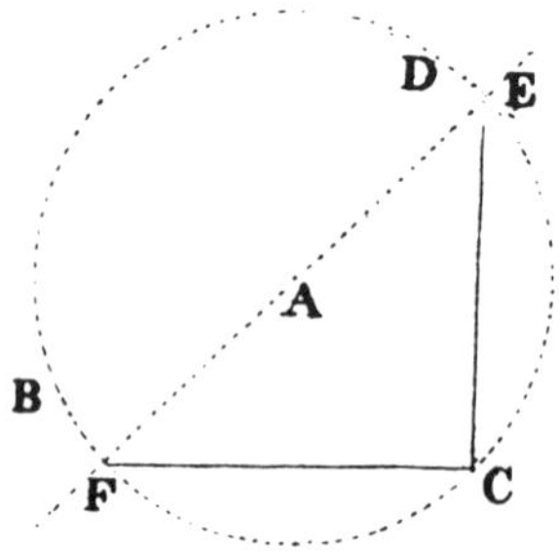

76 (21)

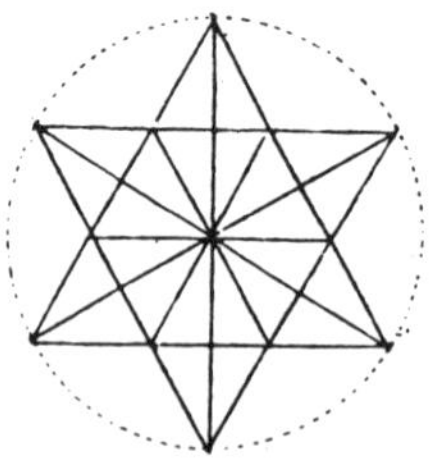

83 (28)

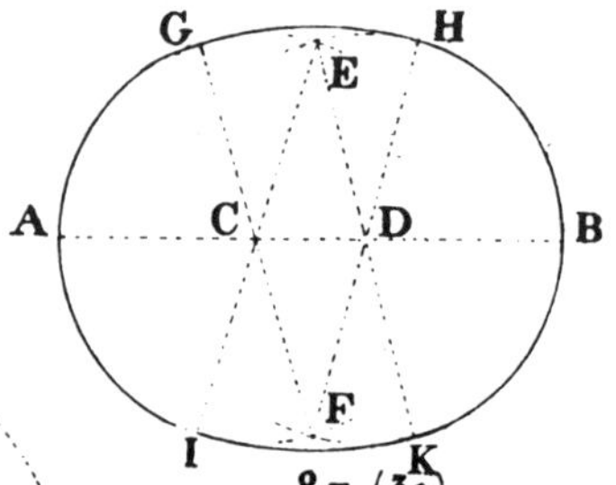

87 (32)

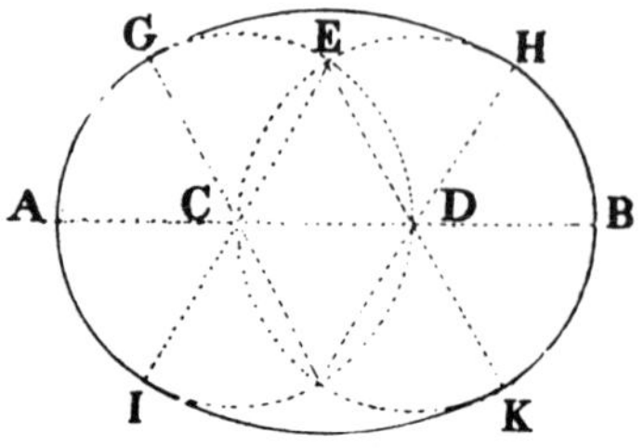

88 (33)

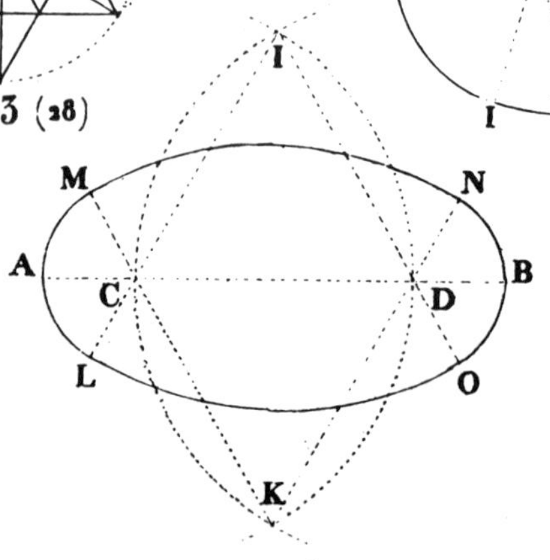

90 (35)

SAMPLE TEST ITEMS

This section provides a few sample test items. It is not recommended they be used in a complete sense with any class of students. They serve only as a guideline for teacher-constructed test items. They do serve the purpose of this book by calling for the processes of higher level thinking.

CONVERGENT THINKING

1. The force required in a 1-pulley system is to the force required in a 2-pulley system
   A. as the weight of 12 oranges is to the weight of 6 oranges.
   B. as the weight of 3 dozen eggs is to the weight of 1 dozen eggs.
   C. as the weight of 1 peanut is to the weight of a 1-pound bag of peanuts.
   D. as the weight of 2 scoops of ice cream is to the weight of 3 scoops of ice cream.

   The above analogy applies to a 2-pulley system that requires the pull of ½ the weight of an object as compared to a 1-pulley system. The best response is A. See Pulleys in the section on Scientific Principles, page 25.

2. Adhesion is to cohesion
   A. as furniture is to a house.
   B. as lumber is to a forest.
   C. as a tree is to sawdust.
   D. as cake icing is to bread dough.

   The above analogy applies to the adhesive properties of cake icing and the cohesive qualities of bread dough. The best response is D. See Adhesion and Cohesion in the section on Scientific Principles, page 19.

3. An Olympic athlete is to a hot air balloon
   A. as a shopper's budget is to a kitchen table.
   B. as a writer's deadline is to an automobile tire.
   D. as a student's report card is to an allowance.
   E. as a cat's tail is to a plate of spaghetti.

   The above analogy applies to pressure, that is, the pressure of an Olympic athlete to compete well and to the pressure of gases in a hot air balloon. This would equate with the pressure under which a writer meets a deadline and the pressure of air in an automobile tire. The best response is B. See Pressure in the section on Scientific Principles, page 24.

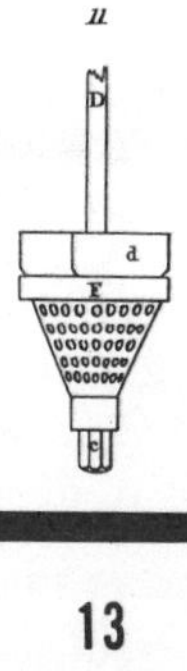

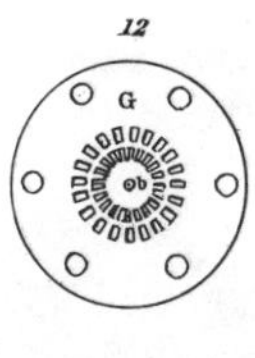

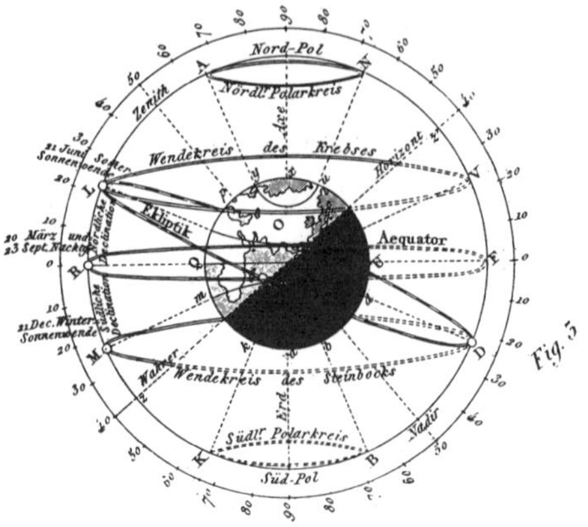

Fig. 5

CONVERGENT THINKING cont'd.

4. Magnetism is to the earth's poles
   A. as bowlers are to bowling.
   B. as tourists are to touring.
   C. as eaters are to eating.
   D. as swimmers are to swimming.

   The above analogy applies to the attraction and repulsion qualities of magnets. Bowlers are attracted to bowling, tourists are attracted to touring, and swimmers are attracted to swimming. Eaters, however, may be attracted by certain foods and repulsed by other foods. The best response is C. See Magnetism in the section on Scientific Principles, page 23.

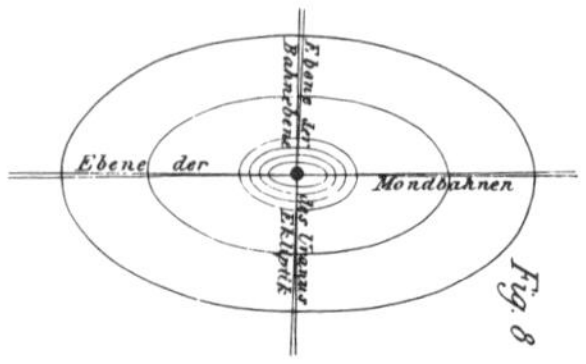
Fig. 8

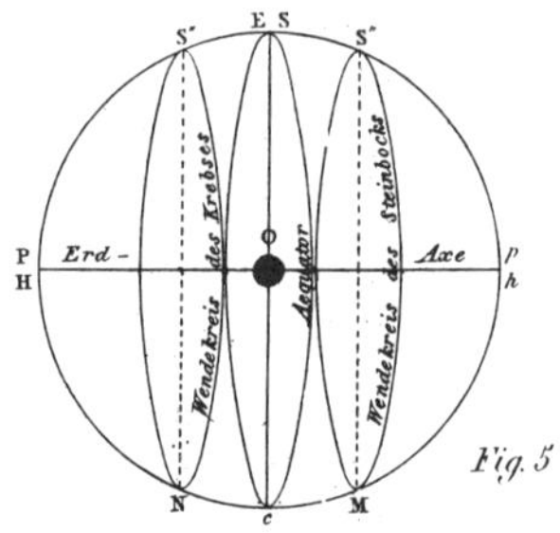

Fig. 5

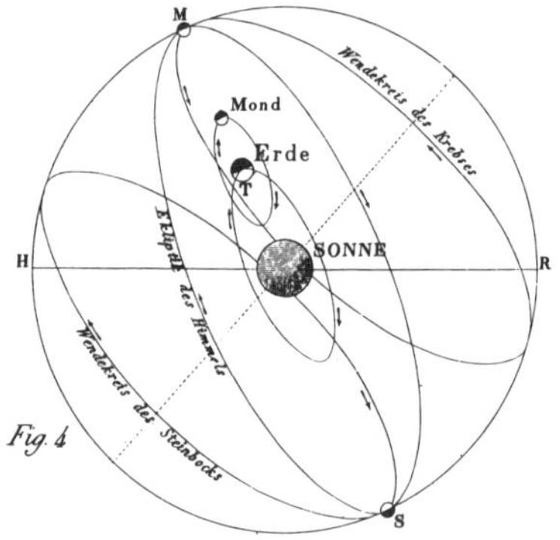

Fig. 4

5. Which is a system?
   A. an electrical system
   B. a pulley system
   C. a system for managing a baseball team
   D. a system for learning a subject in school
   E. A and B.
   F. C and D.
   G. all of the above

   This question calls for associating different categories of thought (flexibility). The processing is similar to that of brainstorming. For example, list all the systems you can. The convergence of thought occurs with the selection of the response. The best response is G.

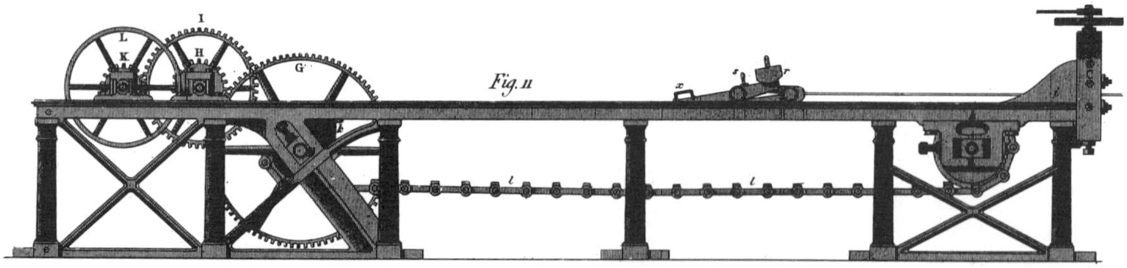
Fig. 11

6. The use of criteria may be applied to:
   A. finding a solution to a problem.
   B. appraising or evaluating the value of a work of art.
   C. maintaining a family budget.
   D. selecting a new automobile.
   E. all of the above.
   F. none of the above.
   G. a few items from A through D.

   This question deals with making application of criteria from classroom inventing to life. The best response is E.

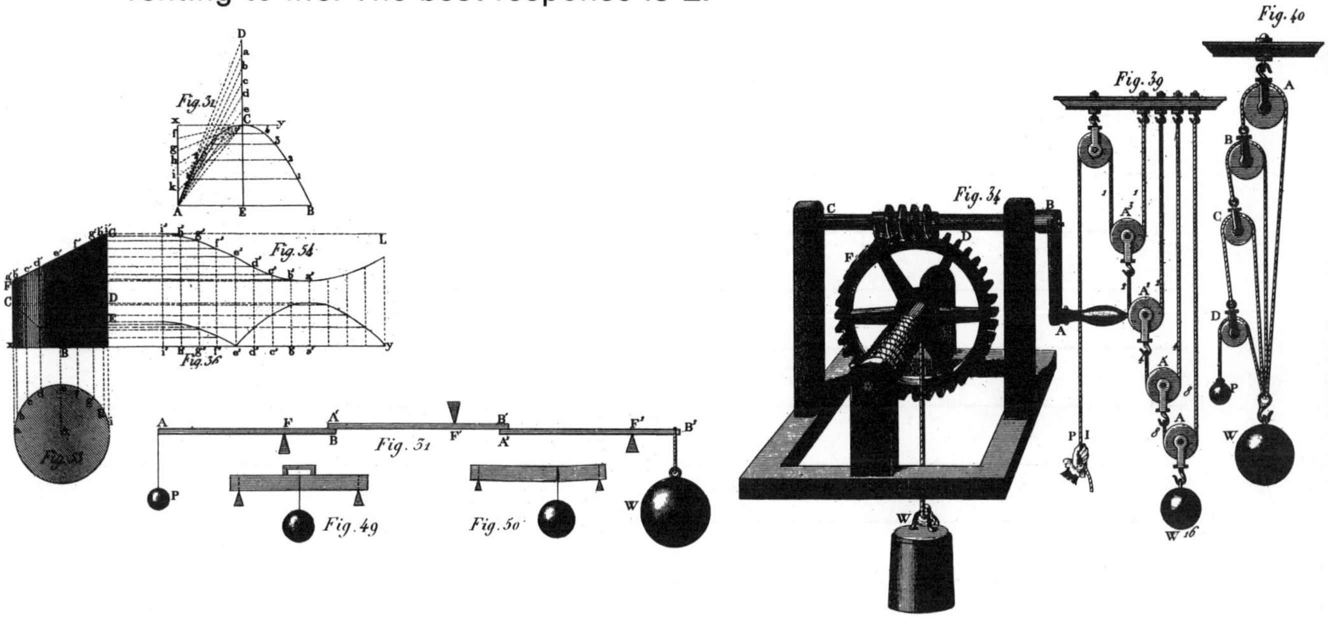

7. Sketch on paper three sequential events that would cause a sleeping canary in a cage to awaken. Event 1 must trigger event 2; event 2 must trigger event 3. Human involvement must be absent from events 2 and 3. Explain how at least one scientific principle was involved in your chain-of-events scheme.

   Students will understand a chain-of-events sequence from the activity Balloon Busters. Assess responses in relationship to the scientific principle explained.

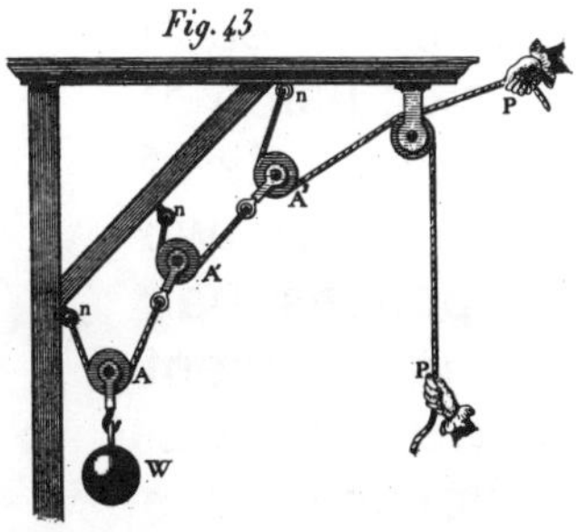

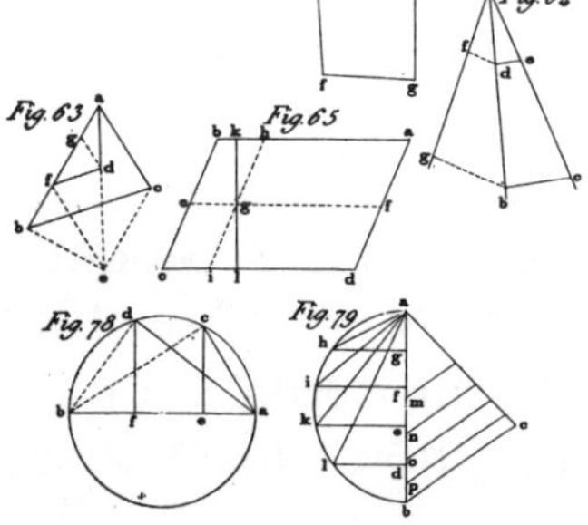

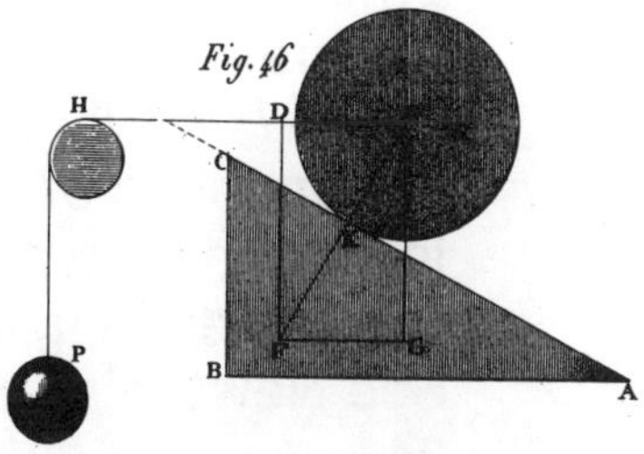

DIVERGENT THINKING

8. Write as many different questions as you can in which the answer to each question would be Newton's Laws of Motion.

   QUESTIONS:

More student response lines will be necessary. Determine a point value for each correct response. Eliminate responses that closely duplicate each other. For example, "What laws might be involved in a head-on collision of two trains of comparable size and weight and traveling at the same rate of speed?" "What laws might be involved in a head-on collision of two automobiles of comparable size and . . . ?" Accept student responses that, in part, deal with the defining aspects of Newton's Laws. Accept student responses that, in part, deal with the application aspects of Newton's Laws. See Newton's Laws of Motion in the section on Scientific Principles, page 24.

9. Either through twisting, cutting, reshaping or combining, list as many different functions as you can for a paper clip.

NEW FUNCTION FOR A PAPER CLIP

A full page or more of student response lines will be necessary. This question applies to the skills learned in the activity "A Coat Hanger for All Reasons." Determine a point value for each unduplicated response. A duplicate response might be: "a hook to hang Christmas ornaments" and "a hook to hang holiday ornaments." As a part of this test item, provide a paper clip for each student.

DIVERGENT THINKING cont'd.

10. Construct as many sentences as you can that you believe to be true about **inventing**. Each sentence must contain two words selected from the list below. In each sentence circle the two words. Any word from the list may be utilized again in other sentences. The endings of the words may be altered or changed to meet the requirements of the sentence.

    substitute
    combine
    modify
    change
    collect
    test
    experiment
    idea

    Examples: Collecting ideas is important to an inventor.
    Changes may occur when ideas are examined.

    ____

    ____

    ____

    ____

This question deals with several things: the concept that creativeness can function best when a structure is present, the processes inherent in this book can be applied, and the interplay of divergent and convergent thought processes is important to intellectual application and synthesis. Should a question of this kind be used, a full page of student response items should be provided. Eliminate duplicate-of-meaning sentences and establish a point value for each acceptable sentence.

Note: It cannot be expected that assessment procedures will relate to traditional grading approaches. Therefore, a grading curve would have greater meaning in assessing and differentiating understandings of students.

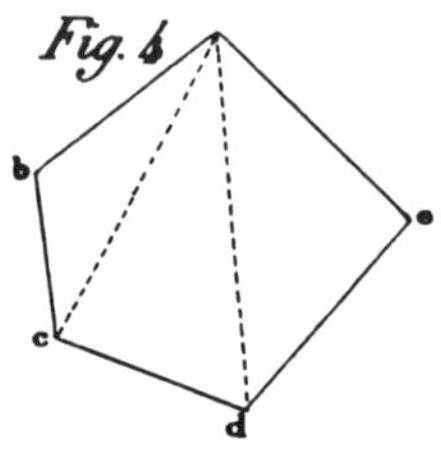
Fig. 6

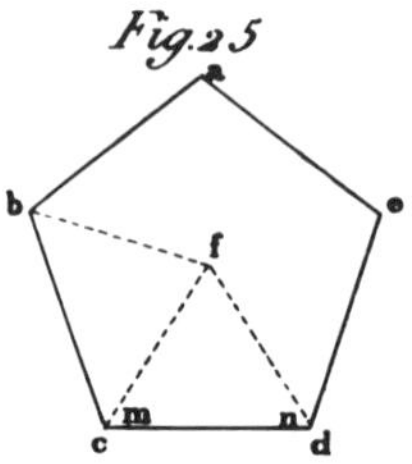
Fig. 25

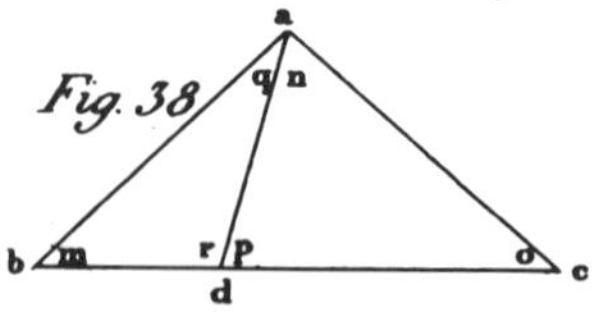
Fig. 38

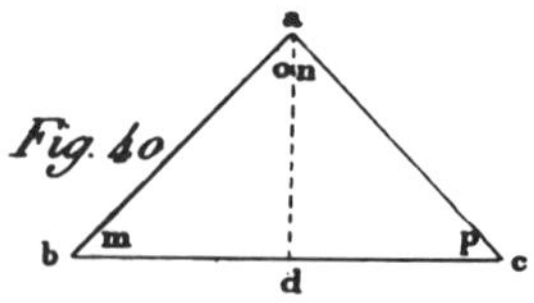
Fig. 40

SCIENTIFIC PRINCIPLES

ADHESION AND COHESION

Adhesion and cohesion are different aspects of the phenomena of intermolecular attraction. Cohesion is the attraction between the adjacent components of a single object. That is, cohesion holds things together like crystals, people, etc.

Adhesion is the same force acting at the surface of two objects in close contact, for example, glue, paper, etc. Adhesion increases with close contact which explains why one must bear down on a pencil to mark on paper and why fine dust adheres more strongly on a surface than coarse dry sand.

BERNOULLI'S PRINCIPLE

When air flows over an airfoil like an airplane wing, the shape of the wing forces the air to move faster over the top surface than over the bottom. Consequently, the pressure on the top of the wing is reduced as compared to the pressure on the bottom of the wing. This pressure difference results in a net force directed up. This force is called lift.

CONSERVATION OF MOMENTUM

Conserving momentum for solid objects is expressed as **mass** times **velocity.** Momentum is always conserved in the absence of outside forces (Newton's Second Law). For example, if we have 2 balls each with a mass of 2 kilograms, this is how we would calulate the momentum in the system:

BALL 1: We assume that it has a velocity of 2 meters per second, so we have:
2 meters per second x 2 kilograms = 4 momentum units.

BALL 2: We assume a velocity of zero if the ball is standing still, so we have:
0 meters per second x 2 kilograms = 0 units of momentum.

To add the momentum in the system: Ball 1 = 4 units
Ball 2 = 0 units
4 units total in the system.

Now suppose ball 1 hits ball 2. After the collison, if ball 1 has a velocity of 1 meter per second or 2 units of momentum, then ball 2 must have 4-2 or 2 units of momentum.

ELECTRICITY

The phenomena we call electricity is the flow of charge. There are two types of charge, **positive** and **negative.** These opposite charges are attracted to each other. In fact, the attraction between positive and negative charges is one of the primary forces holding the matter of the universe together.

The electrical energy that we draw from the sockets in our walls is generated by a system that makes use of the connection between electricity and magnetism. If an electrical conductor is placed in a changing magnetic field or is moved through a magnetic field, a **current** or flow of charge is established in the conductor.

A flow of charge is also available from a battery. In a battery a chemical reaction is used to separate the positive and negative charges. To use the battery we connect a conductor from the **negative** terminal to the **positive** terminal. This conductor forms a path or **circuit** between the positive and negative charges and allows the charge to flow. We say that the conductor **carries** a current. Electrical current is measured in terms of the number of electric charges that pass a point in the conductor per second. Current is stated in units of **amperes.** This unit is named for Andre Marie Ampere, who established the relationship between the current flowing in a circuit and the magnetic field produced by the current.

An ampere or amp is the flow of 6.24196 times 10 to the eighteenth power electric charges per second past a point in the conductor.

In order for a current to flow, there must be a conductive path between the positive and negative charges. This conductive path is called a **circuit.** The "force" that causes the current to flow in the circuit is **voltage.** Voltage is measured in terms of potential difference. Voltage is measured between the points in a circuit. The voltage of a battery, for example, is measured between the positive and negative poles of the battery. A **volt** is the unit of electrical force required to make one ampere of current flow through a resistance of one **ohm**.

An **ohm** is the unit of **resistance.** Resistance is a measure of how the conductor resists or opposes the flow of current. The higher resistance the more difficult it is to move electrons through the conductor.

The flow of electricity in a circuit can be made to perform many useful tasks. This is commonly done one of two ways. The first uses the connection between electricity and magnetism to create movement, for example, an electric motor or an electromagnet. The second way uses the resistance of an element of the circuit to convert some of the electrical energy to heat, for example, the heater coil on an electric stove or the heating element in a coffee maker. If the circuit element gets hot enough, it will also convert some of the electrical energy to light. This is the principle associated with the common incandescent light bulb.

The flow of electricity in a circuit is also used for signaling and control. A common example is the doorbell. When the switch is closed, a path or circuit is completed between the positive and negative poles of a transformer. This path runs through a coil of wire called a **solenoid.** The current flowing in the wire creates a magnetic field in the solenoid. This magnetic field causes an iron rod at the center of the solenoid to move and the rod strikes a chime.

GRAVITY

Gravity is the force of attraction between objects due to their mass. Gravity is experienced as weight, the force that pulls us toward the center of the earth and creates the concept of up and down even though we are standing on the outside of a sphere. Gravity is a concept difficult to demonstrate to a creature born into a world of the up and down. Gravity cannot be redirected or turned off to demonstrate that it does exist. Newton's conception of gravity, while earth-bound, is one of the greatest intellectual achievements in history.

INCLINED PLANES

The inclined plane is really a simple machine. To learn how it works, place a small box on the floor near a table. Fill the box with four or five bricks. Place a smooth board from the tabletop to the floor. Push the box of bricks up the board to the table. Next, replace the board with a slightly shorter board. Again, push the box of bricks up the board to the table. The inclined plane permits a worker to trade distance for force. The longer the inclined plane, the more gentle the slope and the task becomes easier. When the distance is increased, the amount of force required is decreased. But the total amount of work required is the same. Many tools make use of the inclined plane. A wedge is made up of two inclined planes. So are cutting tools such as knives and chisels.

LEVERS

A lever is a rigid bar fixed to turn around a point or axis called the fulcrum in order to gain a mechanical advantage. There are three classes of levers.

CLASS 1 LEVER

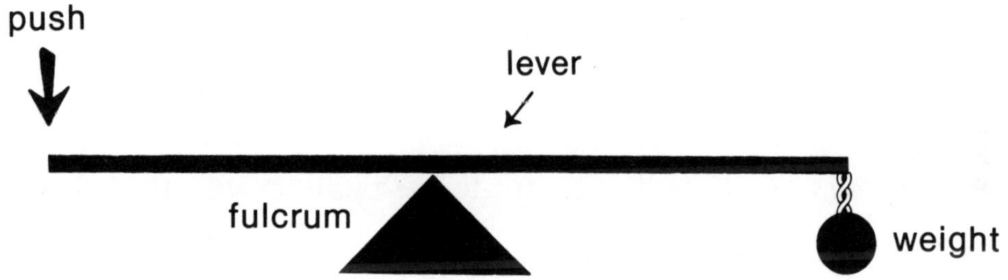

In the class 1 lever, the weight to be moved and the push are on opposite sides of the fulcrum.

CLASS 2 LEVER

In the class 2 lever, the weight and the push are on the same side of the fulcrum. The weight is closer to the fulcrum.

CLASS 3 LEVER

In the class 3 lever, the weight and the push are again on the same side of the fulcrum, but the push is closer to the fulcrum than the weight.

Torque is an important concept with levers. Torque is the ability of a force to set an object in rotation. Torque is calculated by multiplying force times distance.

This is an activity that can be tried with students to demonstrate torque using a playground teeter-totter or seesaw as a class 1 lever. Suppose weight A is a teacher. Let us say the teacher weights 180 pounds. He is sitting a distance (DA) from the fulcrum of 2 feet. We multiply 2 feet times 180 pounds. The teacher is exerting 360 foot-pounds of torque on the fulcrum.

A teeter-totter, in order to be fun, needs to be balanced. Imagine that the teacher wants to teeter-totter with a student (weight B) who weighs 60 pounds. Let us see how far from the fulcrum the student needs to position herself on the teeter-totter. If the student weighs 60 pounds and we want her to balance out the 360 foot-pounds of torgue exerted by the teacher, then we want weight B times distance DB x 0 = 360 foot-pounds. We divide 360 foot-pounds by 60 pounds (360 ÷ 60 = 6). So if she sits 6 feet from the fulcrum, she can balance the teacher.

An additional activity with a teeter-totter dealing with torque and levers is this one:

1. Using masking tape, mark off distances on both sides of a teeter-totter. Use decimal feet when necessary. For example, use 1.5 feet rather than 1 foot and 6 inches.

2. Using a bathroom scale, weigh each student. Each student keeps his weight a secret.

3. Divide the students into teams of two. Try to have student weights as different as possible on each team.

4. Have one of the students sit on the teeter-totter three feet from the fulcrum.

5. The other student then sits on the opposite end of the teeter-totter at about the same distance. This student then moves closer to or further away from the fulcrum until the teeter-totter balances. The moving student records his distance from the fulcrum.

6. When the teeter-totter is in balance, the students switch positions and the second student determines his or her balance distance.

7. Each student has the information to calculate his or her teammate's weight.

   Wm = my weight in pounds
   Dm = my distance from the fulcrum in feet
   Dt = 3 feet (step 4)—my teammate's distance from the fulcrum
   Wt = ?—what my teammate weighs

First calculate your torque on the fulcrum (TORQUE = weight times distance). For example, if you balance at four feet from the fulcrum (Dm = 4) and you know you weigh 65 pounds, then (Wm = 65) your torque equals 260 foot-pounds (torque = Dm times Wm—4 feet x 65 pounds). To find your teammate's weight, divide. Your teammate was 3 feet from the fulcrum so 260 foot-pounds divided by 3 feet would be 86.7 pounds.

MAGNETISM

We are familiar with the common effects of magnetism. Compass needles point north, and magnetic note holders hold notes to the refrigerator door. These examples rely on what are called permanent magnets. Permanent magnets are magnets that produce their magnetic fields without an outside electrical energy source.

It is presently believed that these permanent magnetic fields are the result of the spin of the electrons in the material that makes up the magnet. In most materials, the electrons travel in pairs. One has what is called an **up** spin and the other has a **down** spin. In certain elements such as cobalt and the rare earths are unpaired electrons in the innermost orbitals of the atoms. Since the orbits that are further out are filled, they protect the unpaired electrons in the inner orbit. Instead of cancelling out each other, the unpaired electrons can align their spin and give the material a magnetic field.

Magnetic fields are also created by moving electrons. Electrons flowing with a wire create a magnetic field around the wire. If we know the current in the wire (that is, the number of electrons moving by each second), then we can predict the strength of the magnetic field.

Unlike electric charges, magnets always occur as a **dipole** (something with two poles). In other words, magnets always have both a north and a south pole. If the north pole of a magnet was severed, we would have two smaller magnets. Each of the smaller magnets would have a north and south pole.

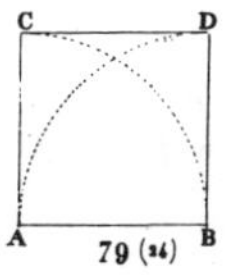

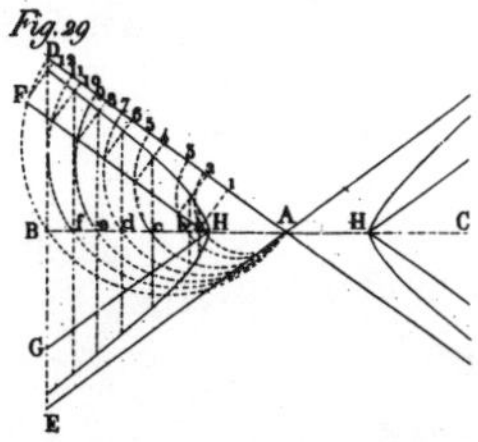

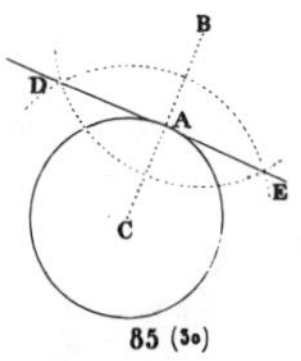

NEWTON'S LAWS OF MOTION

Newton's First Law: (The Principle of Inertia): An object in motion tends to remain in motion, and an object at rest tends to remain at rest unless acted upon by a force. Inertia is the tendency of an object to resist change in its state of motion. This means a moving object tends to keep moving and a stationary object tends to remain stationary unless acted upon by some force.

Newton's Second Law: The changeover time of an object's momentum is equal to the sum of the forces acting on that object.

Newton's Third Law: If object A exerts a force on object B, then object B exerts a force equal in magnitude and opposite in direction of object A. For every action there is an opposite and equal reaction.

Suppose we hang an object from a string. The object (A) pulls on the string with a force (WA) equal to the weight of the object. This force (WA) is directed down. Newton's Third Law of Motion says that the string must also pull up on the object with an equal force. This force (TA) is called the **tension** in the string.

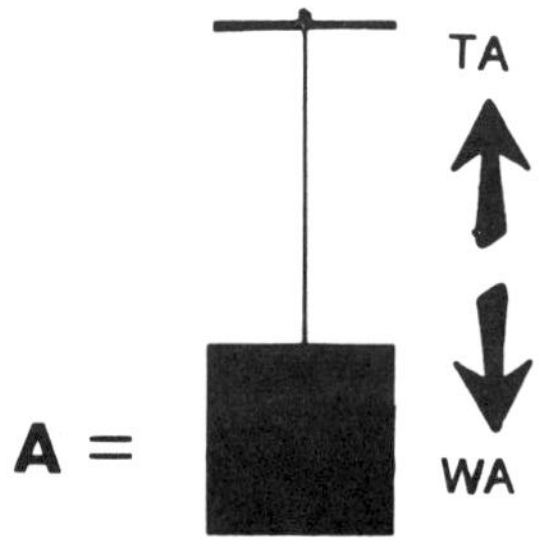

PRESSURE

A complete explanation of the phenomena of pressure is beyond the scope of most middle school textbooks, but we can approach the concept in this way.

Pressure is described as force per area, that is, pounds per square inch. Pressure is the result of molecules being in motion. Imagine a box with a gas-like air inside. These molecules are striking the side of the box. The magnitude of this force is determined by the velocity or momentum of the molecules. The pressure on the wall of the box is the average sum of all the forces from all the molecules striking the side of the box.

If we heat up the air in the box without letting any escape, then each of the molecules within the box is given a high average velocity. Thus, each impact of a molecule on the inside of the box imparts more force, and we receive higher pressure. If we cool the air inside the box again without letting out air, the average velocity of the molecules is reduced. Each impact from a molecule imparts less force to the side of the box and a lower pressure is realized.

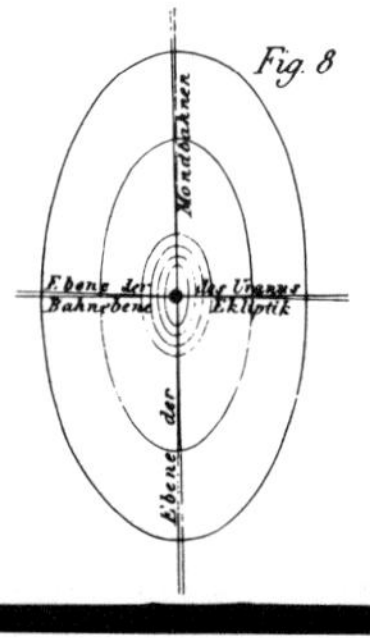

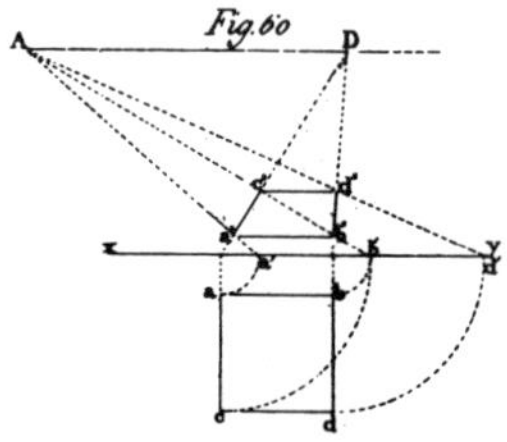

Imagine that we have a box filled with air. We can open a valve on the box and let air in or out. The air molecules inside and outside the box exert the same pressure on the side of the box. Our pressure gauge reads the same pressure inside and outside the box.

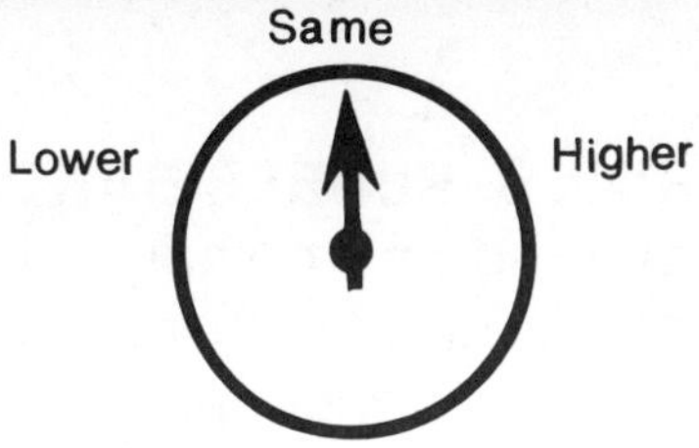

Now we attach an air pump to the box and pump extra air into the box. Having less air in the box will cause fewer molecules to push on the inside of the box than on the outside. Our pressure gauge reads a higher pressure inside the box.

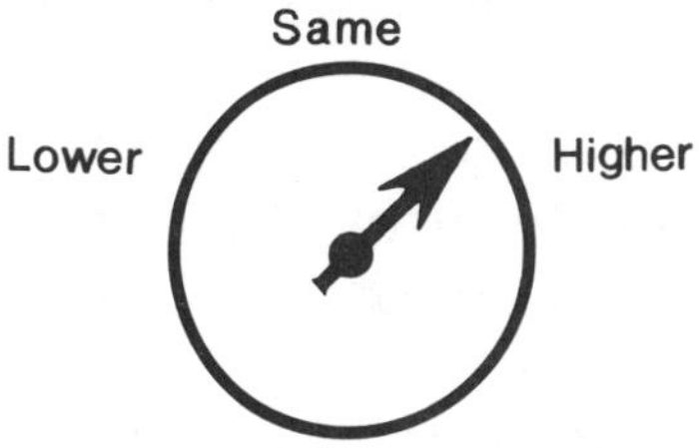

When we talk about air pressure, we usually talk about the pressure being lower or higher than normal air pressure. We can also talk about absolute pressure. In absolute terms, the atmosphere exerts a pressure of about 15 pounds per square inch on everything. This pressure amounts to over 8000 pounds of force pushing down on the top of the average student desk. But since the pressure also pushes up on the bottom of the desk top, the sum of the forces is equal to 0.

PULLEYS

We have two objects, A and B, on a string. Object A pulls on the string with a force (WA) equal to the weight of the object. This force (WA) is directed down. The string also pulls up on the object with an equal force (TA). This is the tension in the string. If we do not want the system to move, that is, to remain stationary, then object B and the forces acting upon it must be the same as object A. Therefore, the weight of A = weight of B.

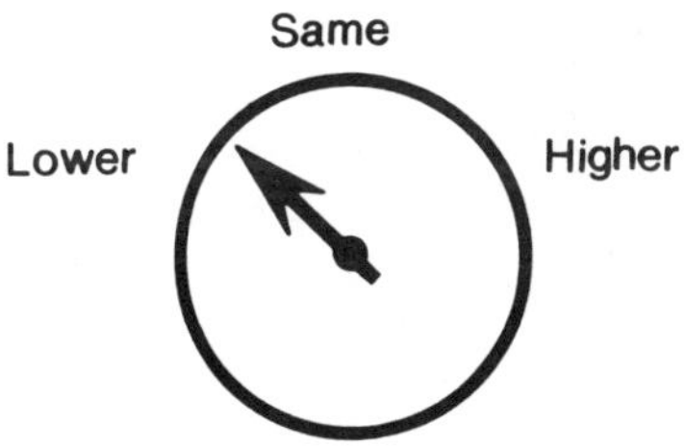

This is a simple pulley system. With just one pulley, the weight of the force on one string is equal to the weight on the other string. If we use a one-pulley system to lift a weight, we have to pull on the string or rope with a force equal to its weight.

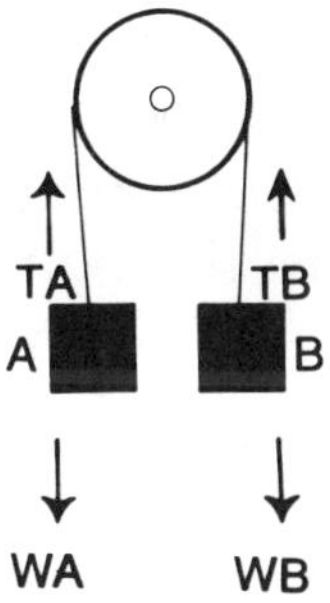

Suppose we use two pulleys. If we look at pulley 1 and weight A, we can see that TO is equal to weight A. See Newton's Third Law. We have two strings holding up pulley 1, and if we do not want it to move, we have to balance the forces involved. We find that T2 = TO ÷ by 2 = ½ weight A. In pulley 2, we already know that T2 = ½ the weight of A. If we want pulley 2 to be balanced, then T3 is also equal to the weight of B (weight of B = ½ the weight of A). So in using two pulleys to lift a weight, we only have to pull ½ the weight on the string or rope. If we use three pulleys, then weight B is ¼ of weight A.

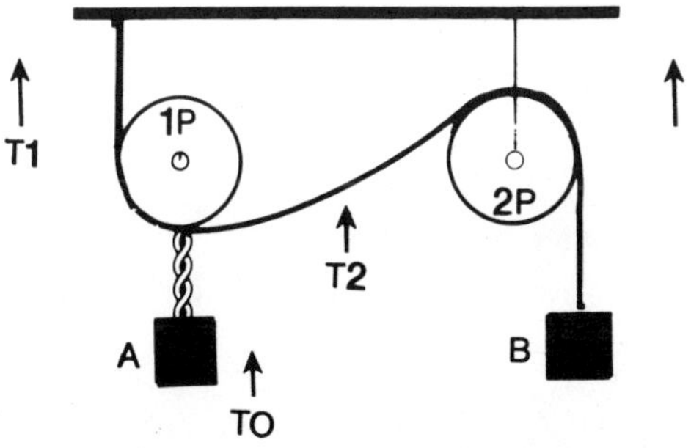

SPRINGS, RUBBER BANDS, ELASTIC, ETC.

Stretching and compressing are explained using the concept of a **spring constant.** The rubber band stores energy by changes in its length. When a rubber band is stretched, energy is stored in its system. The amount of energy stored is determined by the amount of force required to stretch the rubber band.

The spring constant for the rubber band determines the amount of force required to stretch the rubber band a given amount. The spring constant is expressed as force per length, that is, pounds per inch.

Suppose our rubber band has a spring constant of 1 pound per inch. If we begin with a rubber band that is 10 inches long and hang a 2-pound weight on it, it will stretch 2 inches.

$$\frac{\text{2 pounds}}{\text{1 pound per inch}} = \text{2 inches}$$

So our rubber band will be 2 inches longer, that is, 10 inches + 2 inches = 12 inches. Springs work in the same way. Usually we compress or shorten a spring to store energy. If a spring has a spring constant of 10 pounds per inch, then we start with a 5-inch spring and place a 20-pound weight on the spring. It will be compressed to 2 inches.

An example of a spring constant would be the old style spring scale. This consists of a spring with a pointer attached to the spring. We hang a weight on the scale to compress or stretch the spring, and the pointer moves along a ruler attached to the scale. The ruler is marked off in pounds.

Fig. 22

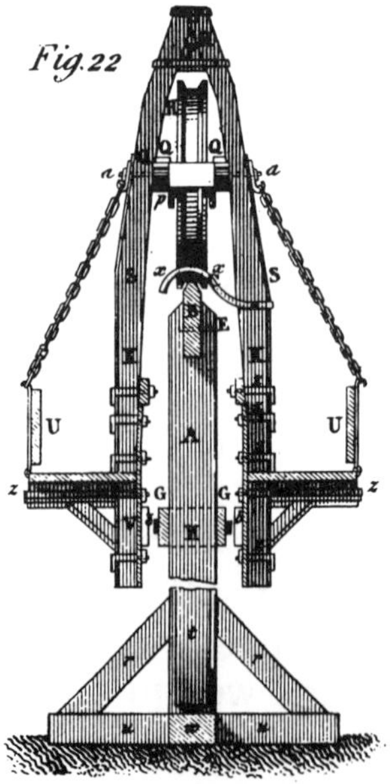

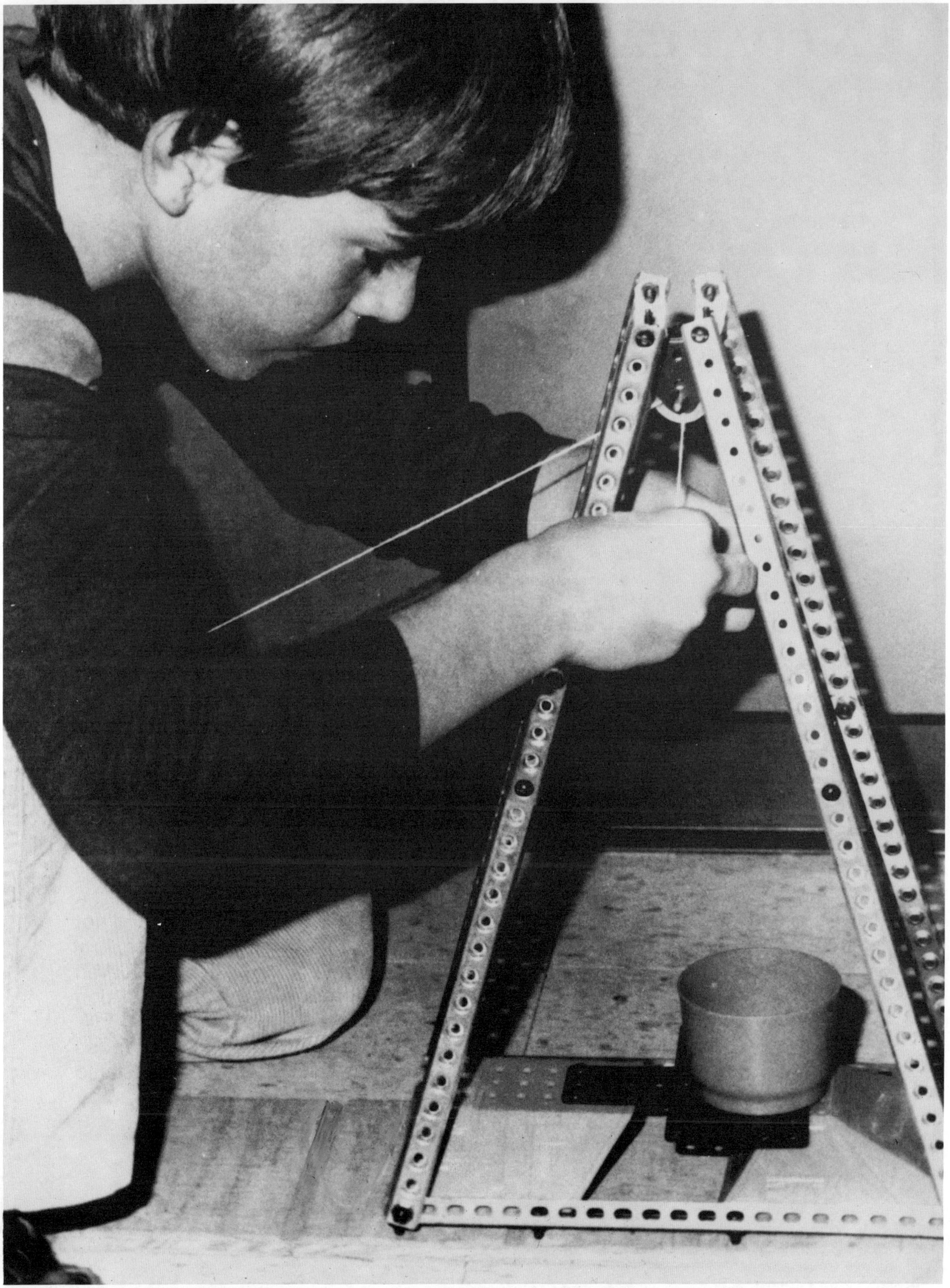

A COAT HANGER FOR ALL REASONS

Task:

Transform a coat hanger into a device that performs a different function or purpose. The device may be constructed in combination with no more than three other materials or objects.

Objectives:

1. Students will transform the shape of a coat hanger and/or place it in combination with three other materials or objects in order to construct a device that serves a useful and consistent purpose.

2. Students will demonstrate the completed device and the purpose for which it was created.

Sub-Objectives:

... Students will brainstorm a quantity of ideas on the question, "How many different uses are there for a coat hanger?"

... Students will list appropriate criteria for selecting ideas that appear possible. (Criteria may include items such as cost, available materials, useful purpose or need, etc.)

... Students will select their best ideas as measured by their selected criteria items.

... Students will construct with devices within the framework of presented conditions.

... Students will demonstrate their constructed devices.

... Upon completion, students may cite the established scientific principles involved.

Conditions:

1. No more than three other materials or items may be used in combination with the coat hanger. A coat hanger may be used in and by itself and not in combination with other materials.
2. A coat hanger may be cut, reshaped or modified in any way. A small portion or the entire portion of a coat hanger may be used.
3. The device must serve a purpose. The purpose may be a useful function. Useful purpose is also defined here as recreation.

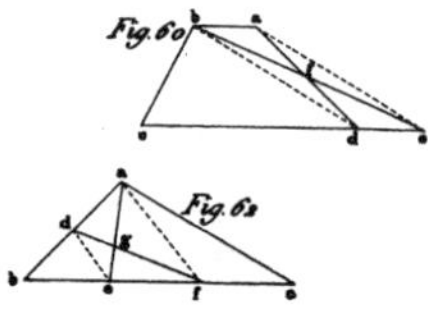

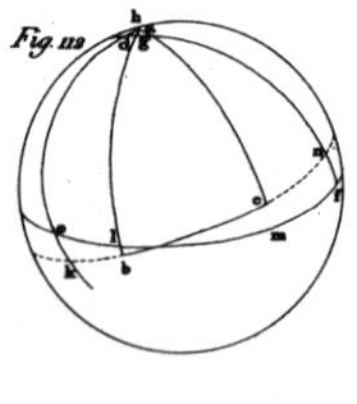

Procedures:

1. Twist a wire coat hanger into different shapes. Ask students to list a different function it might serve in one of the twisted shapes. Repeat the process several times.
2. Do brainstorming on how many different uses there are for a wire coat hanger.
3. Extend the initial list of brainstormed items by using modification techniques like:
   What kind of a shape for a coat hanger would make throwing trash away a fun thing?
   What kind of a shape for a coat hanger would make carrying a baby through a supermarket easier?
   What kind of a shape for a coat hanger would make garage storage easier?
   What could be added to a reshaped coat hanger to make it function in a different way?
   In what ways would a covering over a reshaped coat hanger cause it to function in different ways?
   If the arms of a multi-purpose robot could only be made from coat hangers, what shapes would be most useful?
4. Encourage students to incubate on initial ideas for a day or so.
5. During the next class session, brainstorm criterion items that might help sort out the best ideas. See page 5. Introduce the concept of a criterion grid. See page 6. Encourage students to use the grid with criterion to find a solution.
   Encourage students, while at home, to
   . . . TRY the device.
   . . . THINK of ways to improve the device.

Scientific Principles: Encourage students to find scientific principles associated with the functioning of their device. Have them explain the associations made.

Multi-Disciplinary Expansions

1. Design a jumpsuit clothes hanger. Jumpsuits are generally too long to be hung in normal closets.
2. Create a wire sculpture from a clothes hanger and a block of wood. Identify contemporary artists who are known for their wire sculptures.
3. In what cultures did a clothes hanger appear? What events in human history made hangers a necessity?
4. What kind of a mechanism was used to store armor that knights wore?
5. Determine through a survey of local clothing stores to what extent plastic has replaced wire in clothing hangers.
6. Experiment with piano wire and clothes hangers to create musical instruments. Which designs or shapes were more conducive to sound?
7. Determine who manufacturers coat hangers. In what ways could this information be obtained from stock brokerage houses?
8. Determine the "put-together" cost of a student's invention device involving a coat hanger.

THE SPAGHETTI-EATING UTENSIL

Task: Create an eating untensil for the eating of spaghetti.

Objectives: Students will either

... create an invention
... modify an eating utensil
... find a suitable replacement for a fork
... combine items or parts of items that will prove adequate in the eating of spaghetti.

Sub-Objectives:

... Students will use visual thinking processes in searching out new uses for manufactured items.
... Students will analyze objects in terms of a function they were not intended to serve.
... Students may combine and modify objects for constructional purpose.
... Students will experiment with and test hypotheses of their constructed inventions.
... Students may refine constructed inventions.
... Students will demonstrate the use of an invention.
... Upon completion, students may cite the established scientific principles involved.

Conditions:

1. An ordinary table fork may not be used unless modified.
2. An ordinary fork may be used to place spaghetti into a created invention.

Procedure: Do several brainstorming sessions on *adaptive* and *modification* possibilities to stimulate creative thinking.

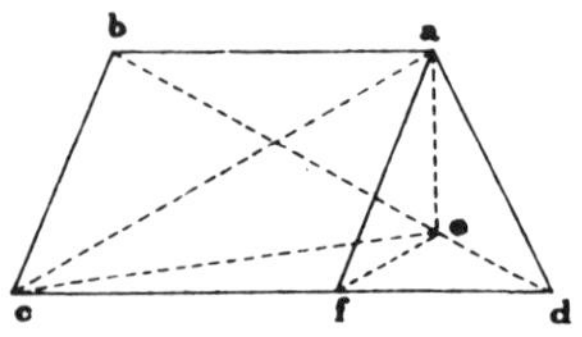

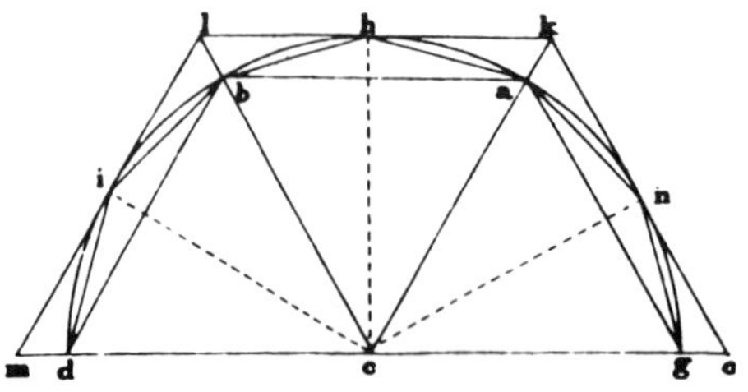

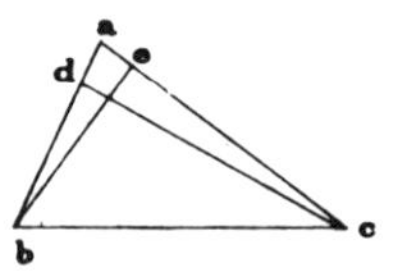

1. In what ways could one redesign a battery-operated toothbrush device to pick up spaghetti?
2. In what ways might spaghetti be scooped? Rolled?
3. In what ways might one redesign a fork?
4. In what ways might one redesign prongs?
5. In what ways might a funnel work?
6. What kinds of existing kitchen utensils might work?
7. What might be added to chopsticks to make them work?
8. In what ways might suction work?
9. What might cause spaghetti to ravel for easier eating?
10. How might a clasp or a clip work?
11. If a chicken wishbone design could be made larger and stronger, how might this work?
12. What could be bolted together for a new idea?
13. In what ways might the idea of a ramp work?
14. What else might work?

Encourage students, while at home, to

. . . VISUALIZE the invention.
. . . MAKE A SKETCH and label the parts.
. . . PUT IT TOGETHER.
. . . TRY IT with spaghetti.
. . . EVALUATE the outcome . . .

OK as is?
In what ways can it be improved?
Need to add something?
Take away something?
Start over?

Scientific Principles: Encourage students to find the scientific principles associated with their inventions. There should be a wide variety of approaches to this invention activity. Consult the scientific principles glossary on page 19.

Multi-Disciplinary Expansions

1. Select some parents to organize a potluck spaghetti dinner. Have students demonstrate their spaghetti inventions along with other inventions they invented.
2. Demonstrate a pasta maker and the recipe for making spaghetti. Encourage students to do it too!
3. Research the origin of spaghetti.
4. Write rhyming poems about spaghetti.
5. Create a collage using spaghetti and other materials.
6. In what ways is spaghetti associated with Italian cuisine and culture? Give a report.
7. Think up some things that could be done with spaghetti that are not in the *Guinness Book of World Records.* If feasible, do one!
8. Create Christmas ornaments using spaghetti, string, ribbon, and paint.
9. Display inventions in local restaurants.
10. Write a story about a spaghetti strand that was allergic to meat sauce.

HILARIOUS HUGGABLES WHO HUG PLANTS

Task: Construct a cute, loveable and soft creature that will hug a plant.

As an optional feature, the huggable may water and/or feed the object of its affection.

Objective: Students will construct and secure a creature to a plant.

Sub-Objectives:

... Students will select, through random search, materials they deem appropriate for constructing a creature.

... Students will adapt, combine or modify materials to create a creature.

... Students will, through their creature design, display embellishment (the creative factor of elaboration) of their product.

... Students may, through invention, create a way their creatures can water and feed a plant.

... Students will demonstrate the function of their created constructions.

... Upon completion, students may cite the established scientific principles involved.

Conditions:

1. The creatures must be created and not purchased. Materials may be purchased.
2. Cost expenditures must not exceed $1.00.
3. The creatures must not harm or damage the plant.
4. Creatures should reflect originality and attractiveness.

Procedures:

1. Challenge students to list things found around their homes that could be used to create a stuffed animal (socks, shirt sleeves, hose, buttons for eyes, etc.).

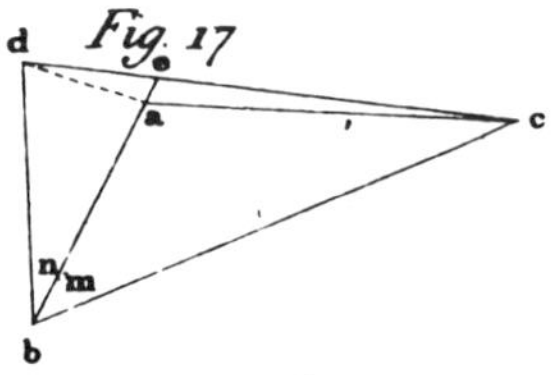

Fig. 17

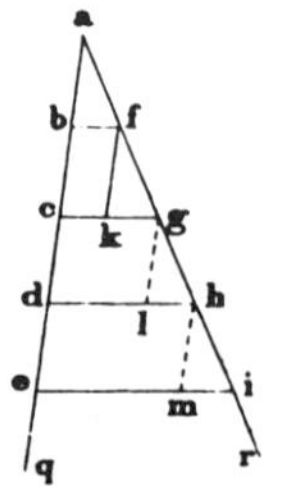

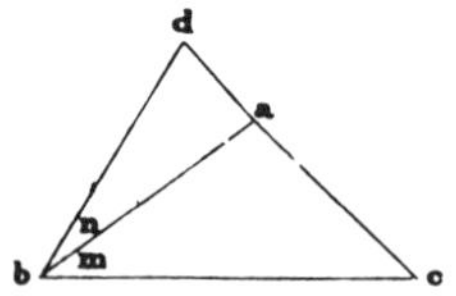

2. Ask students to describe what a dress or clothes pattern would look like. Ask, "In what ways might a pattern be used to create a plant huggable?"
3. Encourage students to draw patterns on paper for plant huggables. Have them list materials needed.
4. Have students list different ways a written message might be secured to a refrigerator for someone to read—adhesion, cohesion, magnetism.
   Utilize the glossary in this book to associate concepts with a refrigerator. Help or ask students to associate these learnings to a plant huggable.
5. Challenge students to speculate how a toy creature might be secured to a plant without damaging the plant.
6. Have students discuss how a system for watering and feeding a plant might be incorporated into a plant huggable.

Encourage students, while at home, to visualize how their creation might function before actually beginning their model. Will the huggable hug a large plant? A stem? The base or the container of the plant? A small plant? A vine?

Scientific Principles:

Adhesion?	Gravity?
Cohesion?	Something else?
Magnetism?	

Encourage students to find the principle associated with their huggables' ability to hug plants.

Multi-Disciplinary Expansions

1. What are the soil requirements for the plant that the huggable will hug?
2. Make an effort to place some of the huggables in flower shops and nurseries. Investigate the possibility of causing some of the huggables to become permanent relics within the school and on plants. Determine a criterion by which the most outstanding are chosen.
3. Make tape recordings of the huggables expressing their love of plants. Take another class on a tour for a viewing and listening experience.
4. Make posters with appropriate illustrations on the importance of plants on this planet. Place posters in conjunction with the huggables and plants.
5. Write one-act plays involving huggables and plants. Manipulate the huggables as puppets.
6. Do attribute listings on the huggables. Which ones had the most attributes?
7. Determine what corporations have associated their company names with animal and fantasy creatures, for instance, Elsie the Cow and Borden, Disneyland (Disney) and Tinkerbell, etc.

8. Determine the various kinds and variety of life found on a single tree in a school yard.
9. Enter some of the huggables in area arts and crafts shows.
10. Calculate the average life of an indoor plant like a rubber tree. Do random surveys among parents.
11. Write a children's story about the plant huggable that became real.
12. Determine by committee the average construction time per student on the creation of a huggable.
13. Ascertain how life would be different if there were no green in the world.
14. Determine how many different categories could be used in judging huggables. Example: shortest, longest, least expensive, most expensive, most colors, etc. More than twenty categories? More than thirty categories?
15. In what ways could this concept be applied to original Christmas tree ornaments? What kinds of suggestions would have general public appeal?

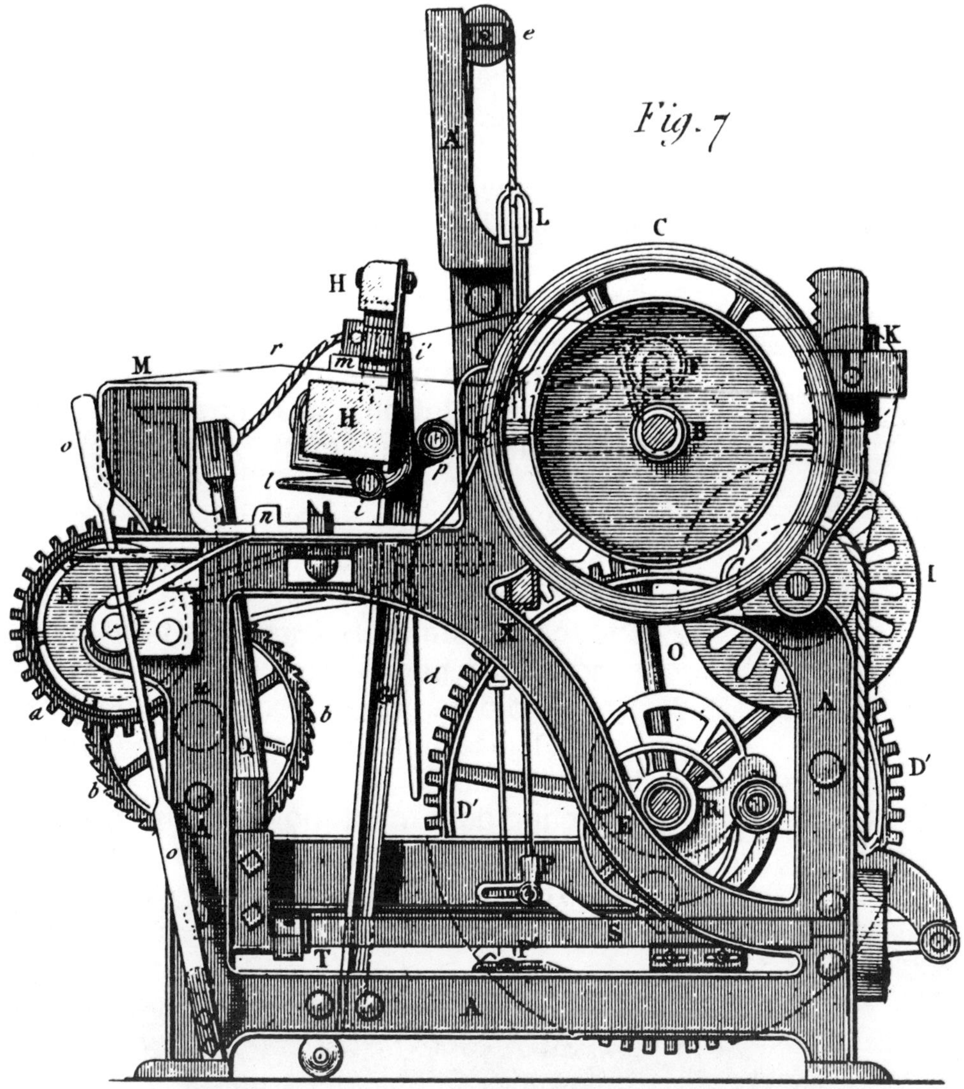

SHAKE HANDS WITH U. NAMEIT

Task: *Create a human-looking device that will perform a set of functions.

***Note:** If this activity is used during a presidential election year, try Objective A. If not, try Objective B.

Objective A: In small groups, students will construct a mechanical political candidate who will

... demonstrate its ability to change positions by moving across a floor area and

... wave a flag with its left hand while shaking hands with a perspective voter with its right hand.

Sub-Objectives (A):

... Students will, in small groups, generate ideas associated with the conditions of the problem.

... Students will be able to organize after-school meeting locations for group work on the problem.

... Students will select ideas from those generated and construct the political candidate within a three-week period of time or less.

... Students will demonstrate the capabilities of their constructed candidate on a date specified by their teacher.

... Upon completion, students may cite the established scientific principles involved.

Conditions (A):

1. The total stature of the candidate must be within the vicinity of three feet.
2. The candidate must wave a flag and shake hands with a perspective voter at the same time.
3. The candidate may perform other political functions. These functions are at the discretion of the builders.
4. The candidate must move about on a floor surface with reduced friction. It can be pushed but not lifted while performing the stated functions.

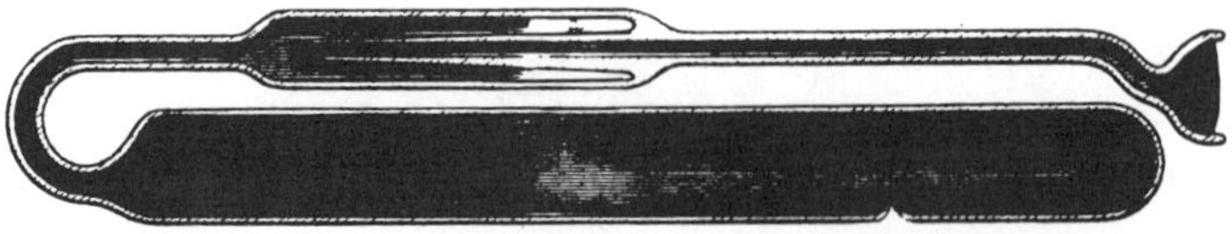

Fig. 3.5

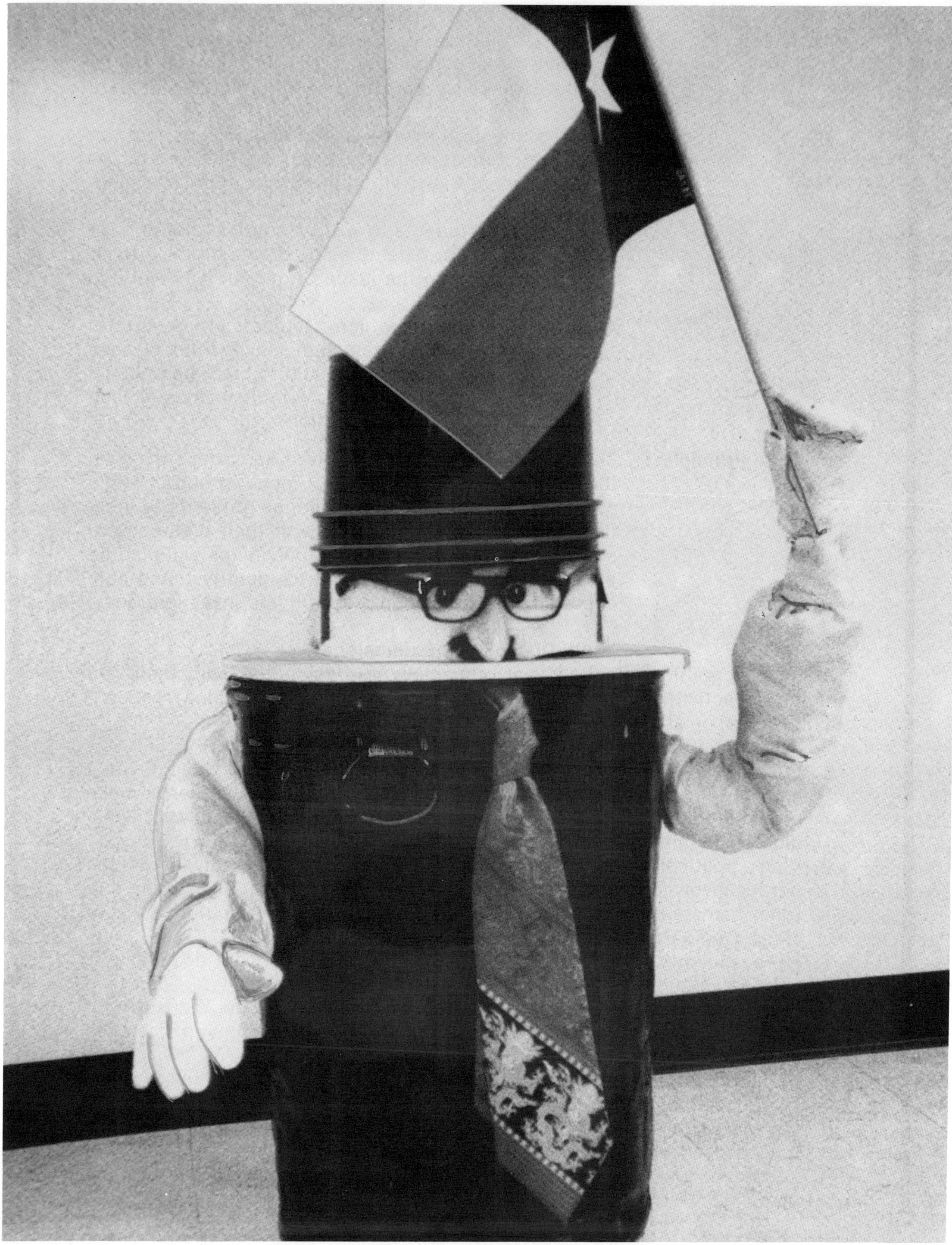

Procedures:

1. Try to organize your class into groups that live within a reasonable distance. This will create some convenience for the home construction of this project.
2. Tell students they may solicit adult advice, but the construction aspects is theirs to do. Should a power tool be necessary, an adult may perform this function.
3. Encourage students to write a political platform for their candidate. What does he or she promise to do for voters? Keep the issue on a national level and not a school level.
4. Establish a date in which candidates may perform their functions at the same time. Invite other classes to observe these functions and to read the political platforms. Distribute ballots with the names of each candidate and hold an election.

Scientific Principles: Several principles will be involved here, depending on the approaches taken by student groups. Make available the glossary and challenge students to identify the principles associated with their created constructions. A number of simple machines will also be employed. Challenge students to identify those concepts employed through research and investigation.

Multi-Disciplinary Expansions

During any political election year, especially a presidential one, there are numerous activities available through teachers' magazines, idea resource books and special publications. We will suggest only a few.

1. Encourage students to gather information on the Electoral College votes and how many votes are assigned to each state. Have students make predictions on how each state's electoral vote will go, that is, to which candidate. Do this before the actual election.
2. Visit a political headquarters in your area, or invite representatives from the parties involved to address your class. Have the representatives bring buttons, pamphlets, and other written information for distribution to your class. Compare and contrast the information received.
3. Have students invent a Trivial Pursuit type of board game dealing with Presidents and presidential elections.
4. Have students imagine their candidates are really running for the presidency. Write a campaign speech that would challenge the campaign speeches of the actual candidates.
5. Do a Gallup Poll type of opinion survey among all students in the school as to presidential favorites.
6. Take a written speech from a candidate that has been published in a newspaper and underscore all factual sentences in red. Underscore all sentences that reflect opinions in blue. Determine what percentages of the speech are fact and opinion based on the number of sentences employed.

Objective B: In small groups, students will construct a mechanical message carrier who will

... deliver either a daily lunch count or attendance report to the person responsible for receiving such a report. The deliverer of such a report will receive a handshake from the responsible party and at the same time, with the other hand, present the attendance report or the lunch count.

Sub-Objectives (B):

... Students will, in small groups, generate ideas associated with the conditions of the problem.

... Students will be able to organize after-school meeting locations for group work on the problem.

... Students will select ideas from those generated and construct the message carrier within a three-week period of time or less.

... Students will demonstrate the capabilities of their message carrier on a date specified by their teacher.

... Upon completion, students may cite the established scientific principles involved.

Conditions (B):

1. The total stature of the message carrier must be within the vicinity of three feet.
2. The message carrier must shake hands and present an attendance report or lunch count to the person responsible for receiving this information. This action must be done at the same time.
3. The message carrier may perform other functions. These functions are at the discretion of the builders.
4. The message carrier must move about on a floor surface with reduced friction. The carrier may be pushed but not lifted while in the process of performing the stated functions.

Procedures:

1. Organize the class into groups that live within a reasonable travel distance. This will create some convenience for home construction of the project. Four or five students in a group is an optimum working number.
2. Students may solicit adult advice, but the construction of the message carrier is their responsibility. Should a power tool be necessary, an adult may perform this function.
3. Establish specific dates for the message carriers to function.

Scientific Principles: Several principles may be involved with each completed product. Make available information from the glossary and from other sources. Encourage students to find the principles they applied. Simple machine concepts will have also been utilized. Challenge students to identify these concepts as well.

Multi-Disciplinary Expansions

1. Investigate the present uses and functions of robots. Speculate on the future uses and functions of robots.
2. Establish a criterion by which the message carriers may be judged.
3. List other school functions message carriers might perform.
4. How many books are classified as science fiction in the school library? How many authors have more than four books in that section? Who are the most popular authors in that section? How many of these authors deal with the concept of robotics in their stories?
5. Debate the issue of people-in-space programs versus machines-in-space programs. Which is more effective?
6. Big Discussion Issue. A book was written some time ago by Antoine de Saint-Exupery entitled *The Little Prince.* It is a story about a little prince and his travels throughout the universe in search of truth. He encounters a fox who wants to be tamed. The prince tames the fox.

   Questions:

   Is the little prince responsible for the fox after taming the fox?

   The fox wanted to be tamed. Does this make a difference?

   Are we responsible for what we tame? Who, then, is responsible for nuclear power plant accidents? Is it the people who build them or the people who receive their energy?

   Who is responsible for job losses resulting in the replacement of human jobs by machines? Would it be those making decisions to use machines? Would it be those buying the products that the machines make?

   What if the message carrier caused an accident at school? Who would be responsible?

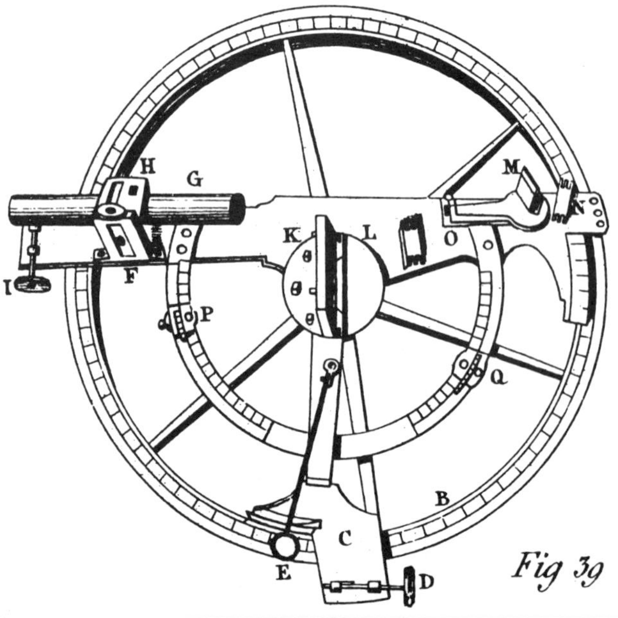

Fig 39

THE PECAN CONTRAPTION

Task: Invent a contraption that will pick up fallen pecans.

Objectives: Students will create a contraption for picking up fallen pecans from a floor or a ground surface.

Sub-Objectives:

... Students will intellectually synthesize and select assorted parts for an invention.

... Students will experiment with and test hypotheses in association with their perceived function of an invention.

... Students may refine or improve their invention based upon performance.

... Upon completion, students may cite the established scientific principles involved.

Conditions:

1. No more than five different component parts may be used in the completed construction of the invention. Things that secure parts or pieces, such as screws, nails, nuts, bolts, wire, string, etc., are considered nonparts.
2. The contraption, when used, may not cause the user to bend at the knees.
3. No electrical energy may be used.

Procedures: Encourage students to brainstorm ideas. Take some of the below-mentioned categories of thought to stimulate creative thinking.

1. In what ways might the concept of a suction work?
2. In what ways might a clasp, clip or prongs work?
3. In what ways might the concept of adhesion work?
4. In what ways might a wire slinky function in regard to picking up pecans?
5. In what ways might the concept of an inclined plane or a scoop work?
6. In what ways might a hollow tube or cylinder work?
   ... a tube with an elbow?
   ... a tube with a perforated lid?
   ... a tube with attachments? What attachments?
7. In what ways might a container work?
   ... a round container?
   ... a square container?
   ... containers with different shapes?
   ... a container that rolls on the ground?
   ... what could be added to a container?

8. What else might work?
   Encourage students, while at home, to
   ... LOOK at how things function that can be found in a tool chest, in a kitchen drawer, in a closet, in a garage.
   ... IMAGINE how things might function in a different way.
   ... EXPERIMENT!
   ... EVALUATE the outcome ...
   OK as is?
   Picks up pecans on the first try?
   Needs improvement—add something, take away something?
   Rethink?
   Redo?
   Try again?

Scientific Principles: A variety of principles may be demonstrated. This is contingent, of course, on the approaches employed. Provide examples from the glossary and encourage students to identify those associated with their inventions.

Multi-Disciplinary Expansions

1. Write a group diamante on a pecan.
2. List other functions each contraption could serve.
3. Create a new recipe for a pecan.
4. Compare the inside of a pecan (the meat) to the human brain. Seek comparative analysis with the hemispheres—apparent creases, etc.
5. Construct a pecan stand. Establish price, record-keeping procedures and profit-sharing plans.
6. Invite a patent attorney to address your class. List the procedures an inventor would go through in gaining a patent on an invention.
7. Organize a pecan festival in which all of the contraptions are in use at the same time. Invent games involving pecans.
8. Establish a pecan tree grove in a far corner of the school grounds.
9. Determine the value of pecan wood. Seek inquiries from cabinetmakers. Determine the variety of products made from pecan wood.
10. Observe a pecan tree. Determine the variety of different life forms that can be found in that tree. Classify those found through research and investigation.
11. Determine what states are the largest producers of pecans.
12. What factors determine a good crop or poor crop of pecans?

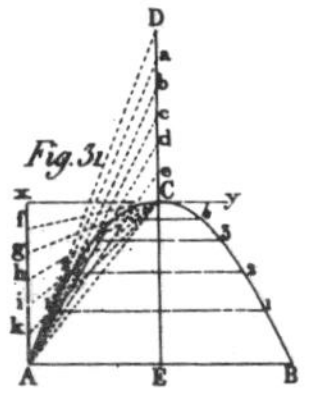

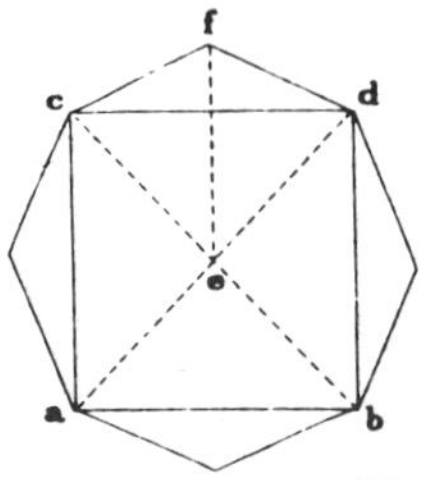

THE BEDROOM PICKER-UPPER

Task: Invent a way to pick up clothes and other miscellaneous items from a bedroom floor without taking a step.

Objective: Students will be able to construct a device to pick up clothes and other common items found on a bedroom floor.

Sub-Objectives:

... Students will list the most common personal possessions they leave on bedroom floors.

... Students will list devices or parts of existing devices or items, if modified (for example, a wire twisted into the shape of a hook and connected to a pole), that could be used to pick up common items from a bedroom floor.

... Students will create a criterion associated with the conditions of the problem to identify those devices that would have application to the solution of the problem.

... Students will construct a multi-faceted or functional device to solve the problem.

... Students will experiment with the device and, if necessary, refine the device.

... Students will demonstrate their invention to others.

... Upon completion, students may cite the established scientific principles involved.

Conditions:

1. The invention must be able to pick up clothing, pick up one item of metal, and one item that is neither clothing-related nor metal-related.
2. The inventor, while demonstrating the invention, must not take a step.

Procedures: Engage students in responding to these kinds of open-ended questions:

1. VISUALIZE your bedroom in the worst state of "messiness" possible. See, in your mind's eye, the debris.
2. List the kinds of things you saw in your mind's eye on paper. CLASSIFY these things into categories like paper things, cloth things, etc. How many different categories?

3. How many different categories could
   . . . a hook pick up?
   . . . a magnet pick up?
   . . . a scoop pick up?
   . . . an adhesive covering,
   like masking tape, pick up?
   . . . a pair of tongs pick up?
4. What categories are left?
   What else might work to pick things up?
5. MODIFY? What could be modified?
   a broom?
   a dustpan?
   a fishing pole?
6. What could allow you to pick things up without taking a step?
   How might extension work?
   How might something that would move you work?
7. Look at the conditions of the problem. Compare the conditions of the problem with some of your ideas. (CRITERIA).
8. Make a sketch of some of your ideas on paper.
   Write sentences about how some of your illustrated sketches might work.

Multi-Disciplinary Expansions

1. Investigate and give reports on the use of mechanical arms associated with the space shuttle and their various functions.
2. Flow chart a way to ensure a clean bedroom.
3. List storage devices that could be used in a bedroom for easier storage. Design on paper better storage units.
4. List needs in which inventions have not been invented yet.
   Examples: A way to get into the kitchen while the floors are wet.
   A way to ensure that eyeglasses cannot be misplaced or stolen.
   A way to sort out junk from a junk box into categories of likenesses, for example, coins in one pile, paper clips in another pile, etc.
5. Design bedroom facilities for a space station.
6. Speculate and discuss what bedrooms will be like in the year 3000.
7. Investigate, through research, the bedrooms of famous people like Einstein, Jefferson (Monticello) and Lincoln (Springfield, Illinois). How are these bedrooms reflective of the personalities who slept in them?
8. Calculate the dimensions of a bedroom. Is the room perfectly dimensioned? List all the reasons possible.
9. Provide an imaginary sum of $7000 and mail order catalogs. Have students create their conception of a perfect bedroom for themselves. Have them select the furniture and the furnishings. They are to design a layout on paper within the cost factors of the project. Provide conditions that the bedroom is 14 feet by 14 feet with one window, four electrical outlets, and a closet of 8 feet by 3 feet. The closet is not included in the 14 feet by 14 feet bedroom area.
10. Encourage students to use clothing items to create a one-act hand puppet show of the good aspects of their bedrooms.
11. Design a bed for an armadillo so that its feet wouldn't touch a floor surface. Armadillos don't sleep on their backs.
12. Investigate five foreign languages for the English equivalent of *bedroom.* Which of those languages are similar in letters and pronunciation? Speculate on the reasons why.

SPECIAL DELIVERY

Task:

Create a device that will send a written message a distance of fifteen feet using the energy initially supplied by a rubber band.

Objectives:

Students will transform the function of items in order to include them in a constructed device which will
. . . catapult
. . . glide
. . . float
. . . all of the above
a written message a distance of fifteen feet.

Sub-Objectives:

. . . Students will identify items that may accommodate the stretching and compressing of a rubber band.
. . . Students will experiment with a rubber band to determine the amount of energy necessary to deliver a written message fifteen feet.
. . . Students will construct a device that meets the conditions of the problem.
. . . Students will experiment with the device and make modifications and refinements, if necessary.
. . . Students will demonstrate their devices.
. . . Upon completion, students may cite the established scientific principles involved.

Conditions:

1. The message must travel a minimum of fifteen feet.
2. The message cannot be rolled.
3. The message must be launched using only one hand to trigger a mechanism.
4. The message must be launched from a surface or floor area.

Procedures:

1. FORCE-FIT some ideas by
. . . brainstorming sports terms, such as bat, racket, shoot, throw, pitch, wind up, stroke, swing, etc. Then ask questions like:
In what ways could one "racket" a message fifteen feet?
In what ways could one "wind up" a message into a projectile?
In what ways could a message be "pitched" fifteen feet? What kinds of devices could pitch?

2. EXPERIMENT with the energy compressed in winding up or stretching a rubber band.
   . . . Use pencils or sticks or tongue depressors, etc., in association with a rubber band. Experiment with rubber band sizes and thicknesses.
3. DESIGN on paper different approaches to constructing catapult models.
4. RESEARCH Bernoulli's principle or airfoil.

Multi-Disciplinary Expansions

1. Create small groups of brainstorming teams. Challenge each team, within a fifteen-minute time limit, to list as many uses for a rubber band as possible.
   Commend the team that had the most ideas.
   Commend the team that had the most ideas that no other team had.
   Commend the team that had the greatest variety of responses.
2. Research the historical development of rubber. What society or culture was responsible for creating the rubber band?
3. Using a rubber band attached to a plastic stacking box, determine how much weight the rubber band can support.
4. If a rubber band was in a survival kit, what uses might it have?
5. Speculate on the differences in molecular structure of a rubber band with that of copper wire. Validate hypotheses through investigation and research.
6. In what ways would a rubber band be like a human tendon?
   In what ways would a rubber band be like a bus full of people?
   In what ways would a rubber band demonstrate Newton's Laws of Motion?
   In what ways would the elasticity of a rubber band be like thinking?
   In what ways would a rubber band be used as a method for counting?
   In what ways would a rubber band be useful in a gravity-free environment?
7. In what ways would a rubber band serve as a burglar alarm to a bedroom?
8. In what ways might a rubber band be made to accommodate music? Art? Drama?
9. Trace the development of the catapult. What ancient civilizations were the first to use them? The last to use them?
10. How many rubber bands would it take to cause a small wooden propeller to propel for fifteen seconds? What methods would be used?
11. How large must a rubber band be to not be a rubber band?
12. How many different geometric shapes could be demonstrated with a rubber band?
13. How many different words have the word *band* in them?
14. How many hidden words in *rubber band*—both frontwards and backwards? Include acronyms too!

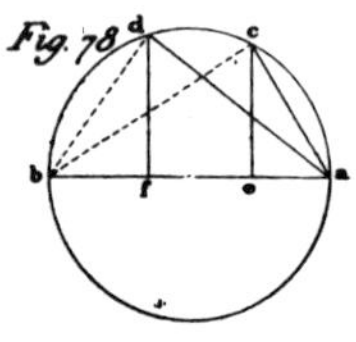

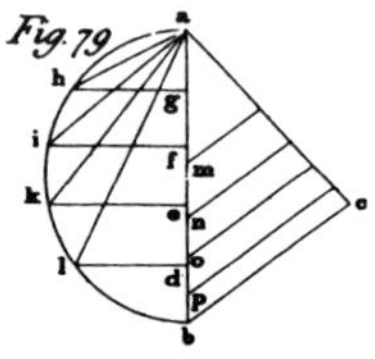

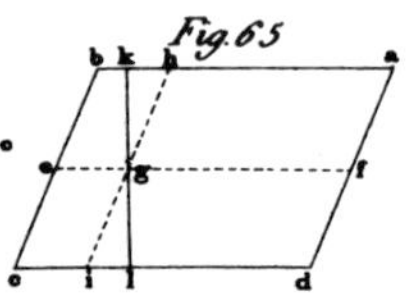

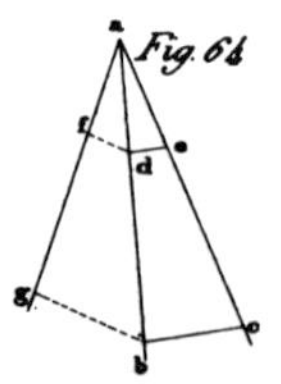

BALLOON BUSTERS

Task: Use the power generated by a mousetrap to activate a chain of events that will burst a balloon.

Objective: Students will construct an invention that will burst a balloon. It shall consist of the following specifications.

. . . It must be activated from the power generated by a mousetrap.

. . . Three different events in a chain of events must occur in sequence. The mousetrap will not be included as one of the chains in the chain of events.

. . . The last event or the third event will burst the balloon.

Sub-Objectives:

. . . Students will generate ideas that would cause a balloon to burst.

. . . Students will converge on one idea that would burst a balloon.

. . . Students will generate ideas that would cause two events to occur which would activate the third event to burst a balloon.

. . . Students will construct an invention that will accommodate the chain of events designed.

. . . Students will experiment with their inventions and refine them if necessary.

. . . Students will demonstrate successfully their inventions using only the power generated from a mousetrap.

. . . Upon completion, students may cite the established scientific principles involved.

Conditions:

1. The mousetrap nor the balloon are considered to be a part of the three events within the chain of events. Three different events will need to be planned and scheduled.
2. An event should be considered as a separate entity. In other words, three dominos may be considered as one event, not three.
3. A mousetrap must be used. No rattraps!
4. Safety is important! An event that utilizes a pointed object, such as a dart, nail, etc., cannot travel a distance of more than one foot.
5. The mousetrap must be a measured distance of three feet from the balloon.

Note: This invention calls for a Rube Goldberg type of response to a problem. Goldberg, an American cartoonist, created bizarre comic-page "inventions" that dealt with simple problems and everyday nuances. He was a satirist who poked fun at twentieth century technology.

Encourage students to really stage an event with their inventions. Each event within the chain of events should be drastically different. After the inventions have been demonstrated, ask students to think in terms of combining their inventions with another invention. If possible, provide an opportunity for doing this. Often, it's the combination of ideas and the compromising of ideas that are the reality of any society.

Important! With younger children, set the mousetraps yourself!

Procedures:

Begin with a reverse approach for stimulating creative thought. Ask:

1. How many different approaches to bursting a balloon?
2. What event could cause one of the approaches mentioned?
3. What event could activate the event mentioned?
4. What event could come before the last event mentioned?
5. In what ways could a mousetrap activate the first event?

During the days ahead, encourage students to continually evaluate their inventions.

EVALUATION:

Is it novel and unique?
Does it work consistently?
Have all the conditions been met?
Is it safe?

Scientific Principles:

These inventions could accommodate a wide variety of principles. Encourage students to investigate some of these possibilities and others:

. . . spring constant
. . . Newton's laws
. . . levers

Multi-Disciplinary Expansions

1. Provide Rube Goldberg illustrations from library books. Encourage students to identify some of the scientific principles involved in some of the cartoons?
2. List other things the inventions might do besides burst balloons?
3. Create an invention title for each invention.
4. Imagine you could write figures of speech you're tired of hearing on balloons before they burst. Which ones would you use?
5. Develop some analogies with the inventions. In what ways is my invention event like a thunderstorm? Like the stock market? Like a flu epidemic?
6. Speculate on what Leonardo da Vinci might do with a mousetrap. What kind of an invention might Newton create with a mousetrap to demonstrate his Third Law of Motion?
7. In what ways could the invention concept be demonstrated from floor to ceiling? In a reverse fashion?
8. Do a flow chart of the invention concept on paper.
9. If balloon art existed, in what ways could one of these inventions accomplish the process?
10. What kinds of accommodations could be made to cause one of the inventions to function as an alert system?
11. How could these inventions be used in a symphony orchestra in the playing of Tchaikovsky's *1812 Overture*?
12. How many different events could one mousetrap activate? Find out with the events created by the students.
13. Illustrate ads about each invention.
14. Demonstrate some of the inventions at a P.T.A. meeting or other school function.
15. Have students assume the role of each component part on one of the inventions. As a group, role-play and pantomime the whole event. Select one student, at a time, to become "defective" during the demonstration. Encourage other students to think of how they could replace the "defective part" with a totally different part.

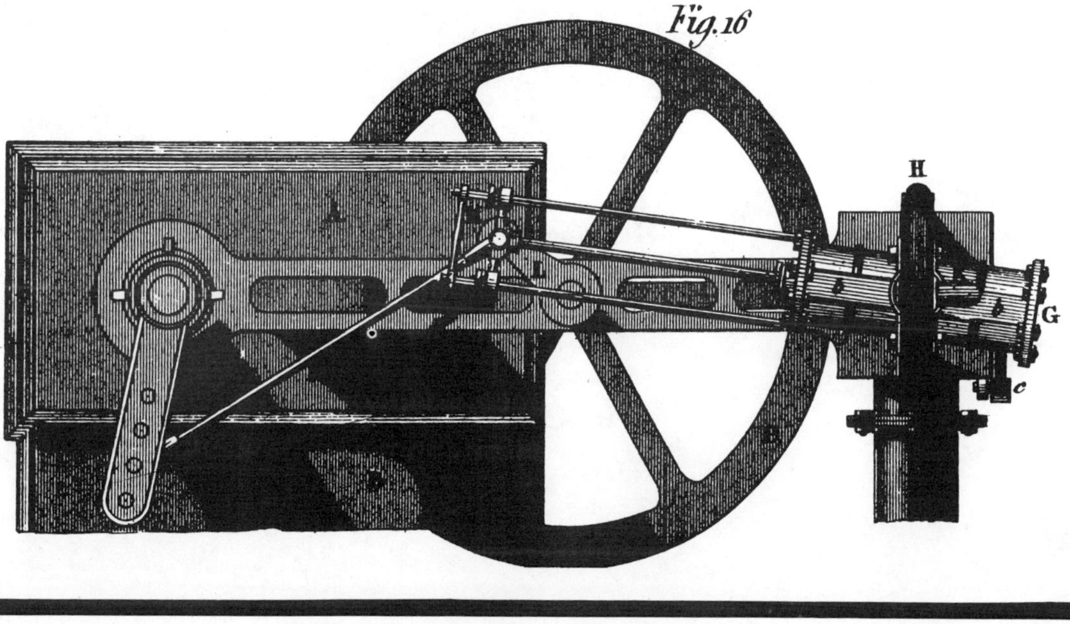

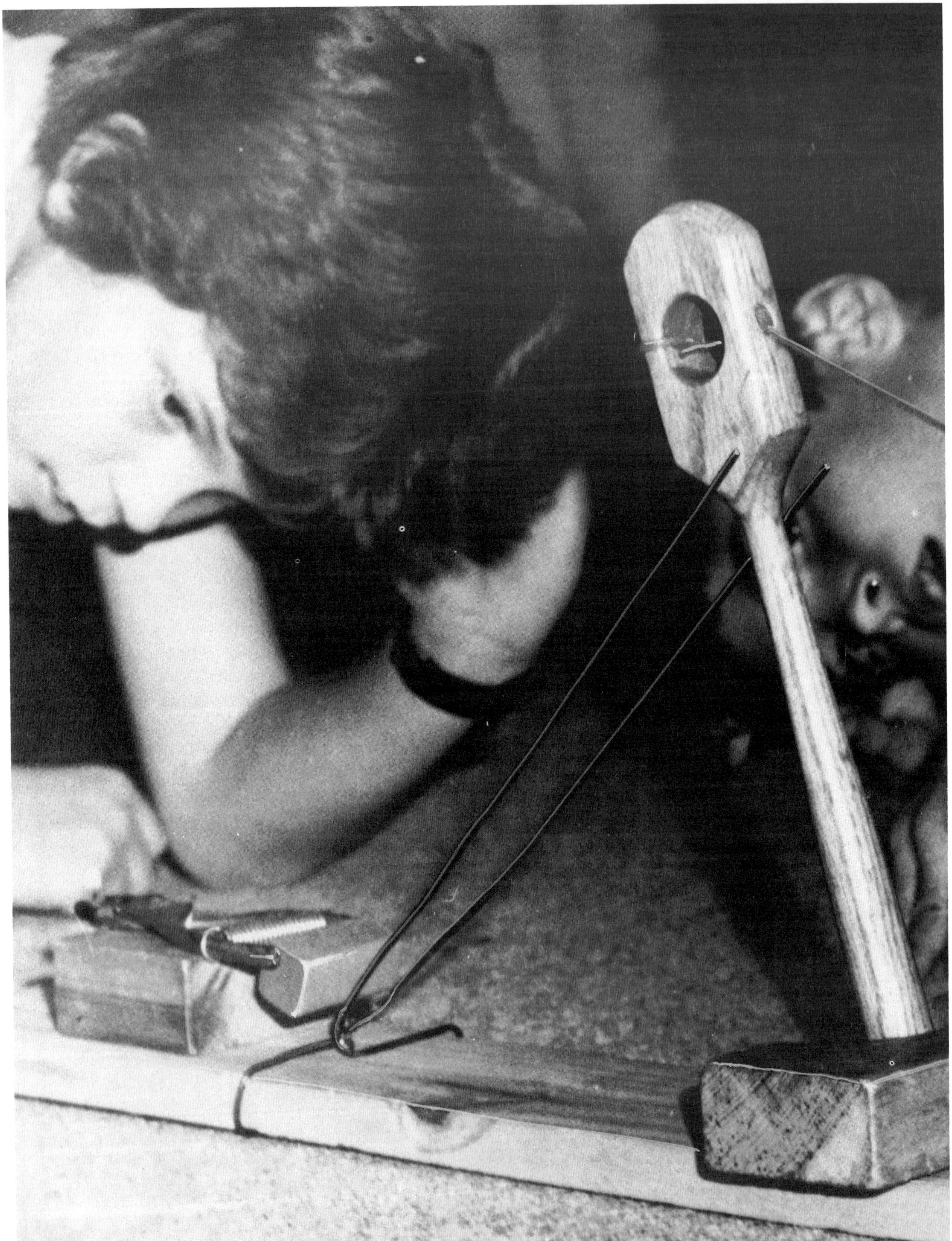

INVENTION TASK SLIPS

The Coat Hanger

Task: Transform a wire coat hanger into a device or invention that performs a different function or purpose.

Conditions:
1. No more than three other materials or items may be used in combination with the coat hanger. A coat hanger may be used by itself and not in combination with other items.
2. A coat hanger may be cut, reshaped, or modified in any way. A small portion or portions or the entire hanger may be used.
3. The device or invention must serve a purpose. The purpose may be practical or recreational.

Date Assigned: **Classroom Demonstration Date:**

The Spaghetti Utensil

Task: Create an eating utensil for the eating of spaghetti.

Conditions:
1. An ordinary table fork may not be used unless modified. Combining the fork with or to something else is considered a modification.
2. An ordinary fork may be used to place spaghetti into a created device or invention, if necessary.

Date Assigned: **Classroom Demonstration Date:**

The Huggable

Task: Construct a cute, loveable and soft creature that will hug a plant. As an optional feature, the huggable may water and/or feed the object of its affection.

Conditions:
1. The creature must be created and not purchased. Materials to make the creature may be purchased.
2. Cost expenditures, if necessary, may not exceed $1.00.
3. The creature must not harm or damage the plant.
4. The creature should reflect originality and attractiveness.

Date Assigned: **Classroom Demonstration Date:**

The Political Candidate (A)

Task: Create a political candidate that will perform a set of functions.

Conditions:

1. The total stature of the candidate must be within a height of three feet.
2. The candidate must wave a flag and shake hands at the same instant with a perspective voter.
3. The candidate may perform other political functions. These functions are at the discretion of the creators.

Date Assigned: **Classroom Demonstration Date:**

The Messenger (B)

Task: Create a message that will perform a set of functions.

Conditions:

1. The total stature of the message carrier must be within a height of three feet.
2. The message carrier must shake hands and present, at the same instant, a classroom attendance report or lunch count form to a school secretary.
3. The message carrier must move about on a floor surface. The carrier may be pushed but not lifted while performing the stated functions.

Date Assigned: **Classroom Demonstration Date:**

The Pecan Contraption

Task: Invent a contraption that will pick up fallen pecans.

Conditions:

1. No more than five different component parts may be used in the completed construction of the invention. Things that secure parts such as screws, nails, nuts, bolts, wire, string, etc., are considered nonparts.
2. The contraption, when used, may not cause the user to bend at the knees.
3. No electrical energy may be used.

Date Assigned: **Classroom Demonstration Date:**

The Bedroom Picker-Upper

Task: Invent a way to pick up clothes and other miscellaneous items from a bedroom floor without taking a step.

Conditions:
1. The invention must be able to pick up clothing, pick up one item of metal, and one item that is neither clothing-related nor metal-related.
2. The inventor, while demonstrating the invention, must not take a step.

Date Assigned: **Classroom Demonstration Date:**

The Rubber Band

Task: Create a device that will send a written message a distance of fifteen feet using the energy initially supplied by a rubber band.

Conditions:
1. The message must travel a minimum of fifteen feet.
2. The message cannot be rolled, wheeled or bounced.
3. The message must be launched using only one hand to trigger a mechanism.
4. The message must be launched from a surface or floor area.

Date Assigned: **Classroom Demonstration Date:**

The Mousetrap

Task: Use the power generated by a mousetrap to activate a chain of events that will burst a balloon.

Conditions:
1. The mousetrap nor the balloon are considered to be a part of the three events within the chain of events. Three different events will need to be planned and scheduled.
2. An event should be considered as a separate entity. In other words, three dominos may be considered as one event, not three, for example, one domino knocking down a second domino, a third domino falling due to the second domino.
3. A mousetrap must be used. Adult assistance may be called for in setting the mousetrap. No rattraps!

Date Assigned: **Classroom Demonstration Date:**

REFERENCES AND SUGGESTED READINGS

Eberle, Robert F. *Scamper: Games for Imagination Development.* Buffalo, New York: D.O.K. Publishers, 1971.

Gourley, Theodore J., and Micklus, C. Samuel. *Problems! Problems! Problems! Discussions and Activities Designed to Enhance Creativity.* Glassboro, New Jersey: Creative Competitions, Inc., 1982.

Isaksen, Scott G., and Treffinger, Donald J. *Creative Problem-Solving: The Basic Course.* Buffalo, New York: Bearly Limited, 1985.

Liem, Tik L. *Invitations to Science Inquiry.* Lexington, Massachusetts: Ginn Custom Publishing Program, 1981.

McCormack, Alan J. *Inventors Workshop.* Belmont, California: David S. Lake Publishers, 1981.

Stanish, Bob. *Mindglow.* Carthage, Illinois: Good Apple, Inc., 1986.

Stanish, Bob. *Sunflowering.* Carthage, Illinois: Good Apple, Inc., 1977.

Stanish, Bob. *The Unconventional Invention Book.* Carthage, Illinois: Good Apple, Inc., 1981.

Torrance, E. Paul. *The Search for Satori and Creativity.* Buffalo, New York: The Creative Education Foundation in association with Creative Synergetic Associates, 1979.

Valentino, Catherine. *The Invention Convention.* Morristown, New Jersey: Silver Burdette Company, 1984.

Vandeman, Barry A., and McDonald, Ed. *Nuts & Bolts: A Matter of Fact Guide to Science Fair Projects.* Harwood Heights, Illinois: The Science Man Press, A division of TSM Marketing, Inc., 1982.